Essays on Astrology

Other Robert Hand books
published by Para Research

Planets in Composite
Planets in Transit
Planets in Youth
Horoscope Symbols

Essays on Astrology

Robert Hand

A division of Schiffer Publishing, Ltd.
77 Lower Valley Road, Atglen, PA 19310 USA

Published by Whitford Press
A Division of Schiffer Publishing Ltd.
77 Lower Valley Road
Atglen, PA 19310
Please write for a free catalog.
This book may be purchased from the publisher.
Please include $2.95 postage.
Try your bookstore first.

Essays on Astrology
by Robert Hand

Library of Congress Catalog Card Number: 82-60410
ISBN: 0-914918-42-7

Typeset in 10 pt. Paladium on Compugraphic 7500
Edited by Marah Ren and Shaun Levesque
Cover art by Stephen Garner
Cover Design by Ralph Poness
Typeset by Anne Drueding
Graphics by Robert Killam

Manufactured in the United States of America

Contents

Introduction

The essays in this book fall into three categories: transcripts of lectures that I have given at various times, essays that have been previously published elsewhere and new essays that have never been published. I would like to be able to say that a single theme unites all of these essays, but that is not the case. They cover a wide variety of themes and are likely to appeal to rather diverse interests. However, aside from the obvious fact that I wrote all of them, they do have one thing in common. They all contain ideas that I wish to convey to the astrological community so that others can react to them, possibly improve on them and make their own use of them so that they have a chance of becoming part of the general body of astrological ideas.

There is a serious problem in astrology. We do not have recognized libraries where astrologers can go and do research on what other astrologers have done before them. For most astrologers if a book is not in print, it is inaccessible. Journals, the few that there are, are to be found in the hands only of those astrologers who have taken the trouble to collect them. I have found that publishing articles in the astrological journals, much as I respect some of the better ones, is not an especially good way to get ideas into circulation. They go to a relatively small group of people and they are effectively out of print almost immediately.

Therefore, I asked Frank Molinski, president of Para Research, Inc., if he would be interested in publishing a book of my astrological essays. He accepted the proposal and thereby gave me an opportunity to bring the ideas contained in these essays to the world of astrology by way of the astrological bookstore. This medium has proven to be the most effective way to communicate with the astrological community.

If there is one thing that I hope to demonstrate in this volume it is that astrologers can encompass both the symbolic and technical sides of astrology. Astrology's unique quality is that it requires a unity of the technical and metaphysical. While I have no quarrel with those who choose to specialize in one or the other side, specialists on both sides must recognize the importance of each other's work. While I admire Geoffrey Dean's *Recent Advances in Natal Astrology* as an outstanding work on the technical side of astrology, I do not think we need comments such as his "There are lies, damned lies and symbols." Astrology is as much a symbolic discipline as a potentially scientific one. (It is not yet a science except possibly an embryonic one. See "On Creating a Science of Astrology" in this volume.) But this lack of respect for an opposing viewpoint is not confined to the technical astrologers. It also exists on the part of the philosophical, humanistic wing as well. I hope that this volume shows in some small way that this split does not need to exist.

The essays in this volume span many years. Some are among my first writings and are not as evolved as I would like them to be. Nevertheless, I hope they create a discourse because it is possible that others may be able to take further the ideas expressed in them. Other essays are lecture transcripts and contain ideas that most astrologers have never really heard me discuss. I would like to take this chance to give the reader a brief commentary on each of the essays, so that he or she may have some idea of the context that each occupies in my thinking.

The essay "The Moon, the Four Phases of the Feminine" is my first work ever published on astrology. At the time *The Aquarian Agent*, now known as *Astrology '82*, was running a lead article on the planet ruling the sign under which each issue of the magazine came out. I was asked to do the article on the Moon for the Cancer 1972 issue. I decided that it was necessary to depart from discussions of the normal symbolism of the Moon, because there was something deeper in the Moon than most astrological literature ever mentioned. At that time, as I am now, I was steeped in the works of Robert Graves, Joseph Campbell, and C.G. Jung. I decided that a mythological treatment of the Moon according to the insights granted me by these authors was the proper path. I am especially indebted to Robert Graves and his writings concerning the Triple Goddess. Other authors, most notably Dane Rudhyar and his school, have attempted to create a system of personality classification based on the phase in the natal chart of the Sun and Moon. I happened to write this article before encountering Rudhyar's book, *The Lunation Cycle*, but I do not feel that his work either obsoletes or contradicts this essay. I am not completely happy with any of the existing work on lunation types, including my own work. However, I feel that a complete understanding of the mythic basis of the lunation cycle is necessary in order to create a lunation typology.

"The Wave Theory of Astrology" is published here for the first time, but it is a transcript of a lecture given in 1973 to the National Council for Geocosmic Research in New York City. It was the product of my first encounter with John Addey. I realized that his harmonic viewpoint contained within it the seeds of a revolutionary understanding of astrology, but as I saw it at the time, Addey had been concentrating primarily on harmonics as divisions of space. I immediately saw that where there are harmonics, there must be waves, i.e. cycles. Since then I have come to realize that Addey's perception of the wave aspect of astrology was more like my own than I saw it at that time. However, this essay is a discussion of a possible model for astrological influence and contains some ideas borrowed from information theory and music. I would by no means offer this as the last word on the subject. It is not even *my* last word, but I believe that there is merit to the basic approach described in the essay. Geoffrey Dean refers to this essay in *Recent Advances in Natal Astrology* and offers some criticisms of it. I am not entirely satisfied with his criticisms, but welcome the opportunity for the astrological community to judge who is right and who is wrong.

The essay is a verbatim transcript of the lecture. Therefore, it is not especially polished. I ask for the reader's indulgence.

"Mercury, the Modulator" is the result of my efforts to come to a core understanding of the major astrological symbols. My book *Horoscope Symbols* is the culmination of this effort. However, this essay represents my effort to deal with the essentially trivial delineations of the planet Mercury in most astrological literature. Reading Jung's works on alchemy, it became clear to me that Mercury was a vastly underrated symbol in astrology. It has a great deal to do with determining the structure of reality and has a strong organic connection with Saturn. This is a considerable departure from the trivial messenger-boy-of-the-gods image of Mercury to which most astrologers cling. The basic ideas contained in this essay have been carried over into *Horoscope Symbols* but the connection with alchemy is much more explicit in this essay than in the book.

"Handling the Malefics" is also a transcript of a lecture. It appeared in *Kósmos* recently. As with all lectures, it was written to be heard, not read, but it does represent some of my most current thoughts on the subject of handling difficult planetary energies. In it I describe behavioral strategies for dealing with the so-called malefics, although I do not make light of the difficulty that these energies can present in life.

"Geocentric Latitude: Some Second Thoughts" is a purely technical discussion of issues that I consider to be major problems among technically oriented astrologers. The consequences of using or not using geocentric latitude in computing houses are not great. The chart will be functionally identical in either case. However, this essay does present what I believe to be an original solution to the problem of finding the horizon for persons born on mountains or in deep valleys. It even offers a solution to finding the horizon of persons born in an orbital satellite. Of course, this is academic until someone is actually born in one. This is discussed in a postscript, which was written especially for this book.

"On Creating a Science of Astrology" is an essay that I believe to be of some importance for the understanding of astrology as a discipline. It is of no relevance to practical astrological counselling, but it will be useful if the reader ever gets caught in a discussion as to whether astrology is a science or not. It was originally written as a letter to *The Humanist*, the magazine that published the condemnation of astrology by the infamous 186 scientists. It was printed in part in the magazine, but it was heavily edited. It was reprinted in its entirety in the *Journal of Geocosmic Research*. It is this version that appears here.

"A New Approach to Transits" is a discussion of transits by means of parans, or planetary co-transits of the angles. The technique is quite complex, but with the advent of microcomputers, it is not beyond the reach of researchers. The actual methods of computing the paran positions given in this article are not the ones I currently use. The changes are given in an addendum to the article. However, the method explained in the main body of the article is completely correct, just a bit harder to use. I do not feel that paran transits should be used instead of ecliptic transits, but I think that they do serve to show another dimension of the transit issue. Tentatively, I might suggest that paran transits show externally caused events (i.e. events that *seem* especially to be externally caused) rather than events directly and clearly caused by one's own actions. The two cases given are remarkable in that there do not seem to be very many clear transits in the conventional framework of the ecliptic.

"Crises of Human Growth" is a discussion of the major periods of life-crisis in adult development. These are important in that they coincide with those found by psychologists, independent of astrology, and yet the symbolism is completely derived from astrology. If you have read Gail Sheehy's book *Passages* you will see a strong connection. It should be noted that my article is completely based on observations formulated prior to the publication of her book.

"Astrology's Second Dimension" is another technical discussion involving the geometrical movement of planets in the houses and with respect to the angles. The problem dealt with here is the one of astrologers using only the dimension of longitude in locating a planet in the chart. Even those astrologers who do use a vertical dimension in astrology, use declination. I do not quarrel with the use of declination, but it is always used independently of longitude. This essay suggests the use of latitude and longitude together, latitude being the vertical counterpart of longitude rather than declination, which corresponds to right ascension on the equator.

"Symbols of the Father Complex" is a concise version of material that will appear in much more expanded form in a forthcoming book. This is also a direct transcription of a lecture. One of its significant features is the incorporation of Jupiter into the symbols of the father complex, giving it a clear role in human development. Most treatments of Jupiter are rather superficial, never going beyond its being the so-called "Greater Benefic."

"Dodekatemoria: An Ancient Greek Technique" is a new essay, but it has been delivered in lecture form. However, this is not a transcript. This is the original essay upon which the lectures have been based. It is a discussion of an ancient Greek technique by which each planet is associated with another position called its dodekatemorion or twelfth place. The article discusses both the history of the method and the surprising way that it seems to work in modern charts. It should be interesting for those who believe harmonic astrology is a new approach. These positions turn out to be based on harmonic principles used over two thousand years ago.

"The Ascendant, Midheaven and Vertex in Extreme Latitudes" continues with issues begun in the essay on geocentric latitude. This essay was originally written for Charles Jayne's *Cosmecology Bulletin*. However, various considerations prevented him from publishing the issue in which it was to have appeared. The material that appears in this essay is definitely theoretical, but it does have consequences for certain practices normally employed by astrologers, such as the use of the Vertex in tropical latitudes. Again the problems with the Ascendant and Midheaven in the Arctic turn out to be due to the fact that astrologers have not been clear about the precise definitions of these points. The conventional definitions work fine in temperate latitudes, but break down completely in the Arctic, Antarctic and, in the case of the Vertex, tropical latitudes. Not all of the paradoxical qualities of these points in the Arctic, Antarctic and tropics can be resolved. However, sense can be introduced into the matter by the use of consistent definitions.

"The Age and Constellation of Pisces" is a previously unpublished essay that explores the astrology of historical periods. It also employs a new way of looking at the figures of the constellations as mythic images describing the psychic evolution of the cultures that perceive them. Although technical methods are employed to get at the material, this is not primarily a technical essay. It is primarily philosophical, psychological and historical. There are very strong implications in this material for the future of our civilization. I think that this is also a more satisfactory format for dealing with the whole issue of the Piscean and Aquarian Ages. I have given lectures based on this material on several occasions in recent months and they have been well received. I believe that this article is a particularly good example of the fusion of humanistic and technical astrology. The conclusions of this article are definitely related to the development of human consciousness and yet this could not have been done without a computer. This should serve notice to those who do not believe in the ability of computers to expand astrological awareness.

In essence, the kind of fusion that this essay achieves is part of what I talked about earlier—the radical breakthroughs that can be achieved through the combination of the art with the technology of astrology. I can only hope that the availability of these essays will assist others in achieving this synthesis.

1

The Moon,
the Four Phases of the Feminine

The Moon, one of the three important centers of the horoscope, is at the same time one of the least clearly understood factors in the chart, or, at least, it is poorly communicated by most astrological textbook authors. Granted that this may seem like an extraordinary statement to the many astrologers who use the Moon in delineating charts and achieve good results, but the results are consistently of a very superficial kind or, when not, are couched in the technical phrasing of Theosophy or some similar system. Very seldom do we see the Moon clearly analyzed in terms of the psychological, mythical depths of the symbol.

If astrology is to evolve, we must get beyond the crude, exoteric, fortune-telling orientation inherited from the past and begin to come to terms with the symbols in a new kind of way. We must learn to *feel* the symbolism and not merely relate to its surface. We must see the symbols, and the world through them. In fact we must become possessed by them, much the way the ancients were by their gods. This is not a call for all astrologers to become insane in order to understand truly what they are about, but more dangerous journeys in life and understanding are called for than most students of astrology have undergone. We are students of the archetypal symbolism of Being itself, as reflected in the planets. This is the task and we must proceed with the importance of this in our minds at all times.

So who or what is the Moon? Is she the soul, the personality, the ego, or the self, we ask, as if even these terms were clearly understood in the same way by all astrologers. We try very hard to reduce the Moon to the terms of our own experience but we do not ask if our experience here in the late twentieth century is adequate to encompass the archetype represented by the Moon. Why not? We all have the Moon in our horoscopes and therefore the lunar symbolism ought to be operative in our lives.

A clue is given by some astrologers who consider the Moon to be a symbol of the unconscious mind. This is the problem. It is not that the Moon is inherently unconscious, as these authors suggest, but the Moon represents a function of the psyche that is repressed in our culture and has been for some time. While the lunar function operates in our lives, we are largely unaware of exactly how it operates. (Possibly this is less true of women than of men; see below.)

But this has not always been the case. The ancients worshipped all manner of feminine deities, most of whom were connected with the Moon in some way. So generally was this the case, it would appear that the Moon was the general symbol of the archetypal feminine, which all of these goddesses represented in various ways.

Here, then, is the core of the problem. The Moon represents the archetype of femininity itself, or in Chinese philosophy, Yin. All of the other delineations and interpretations arise out of this basic fact.

Taoism teaches that existence arises out of a continual interplay between the archetypal feminine, Yin, and the archetypal masculine, Yang. The two are equal and coordinate principles of the One. In order for the One to achieve manifestation, it must create the illusion of the Two, hence Yin and Yang.

However, almost all of the descriptions of the archetypal feminine have been given to us by patriarchal cultures, of which our own is one, cultures that are overwhelmingly dominated by the archetypal masculine. Therefore the feminine is usually described in negative terms as a collection of non-masculine traits. Yin is yielding, passive, receptive, dark, material (as opposed to spiritual) and inferior. If Yin and Yang are equal principles of Being, then Yang is at least the "more equal" of the two, according to these descriptions.

In our own culture we are in even rougher shape trying to understand the nature of the archetypal feminine because the dominant religions, Christianity and Judaism, have completely thrown the archetypal feminine out of Western religion. The feminine simply remains as part of "the snare of the Devil." Ever wondered why God is "He"?

The archetypal feminine in our culture has been repressed until it survives only as an inferior, "dark" function, moods, feelings, unconscious drives, etc. According to Depth Psychologists, whenever a function becomes repressed in this way, it becomes dangerous. It goes out of the control of the conscious mind and gains an energy of its own by means of which it can assault the seat of consciousness. Kindly note that the old term for insanity is "lunacy." To be insane was to be "moon-struck," because the

Moon somehow caused insanity. Sleeping in the light of the full Moon was also believed to cause a person to lose his or her mind. I do not believe that this is because the Moon rules the emotions, as most astrologers assert, but because the Moon represents a repressed function of the psyche. The full Moon especially is a time when the archetypal feminine stands out most clearly as the polar opposite and complement of the archetypal masculine, represented by the Sun. More on this a bit farther on!

Lunacy or insanity represents the same principle that the ancients believed in when they said that any god or goddess who was not worshipped properly would drive the offenders mad. Lunacy represents the revenge of the repressed lunar function upon the conscious mind. That insanity is connected with the Moon is not so much due to the intrinsic nature of the Moon as it is to its status as a repressed function. And of course for the male-female polarity correctly to operate in our lives both of them must be functioning properly. The clear implication of this is that the archetypal masculine is not in such great shape either. And I believe there is a solar insanity among us that has not received enough attention.

I attribute the rise of the long-overdue woman's liberation movement to the repression of the archetypal feminine.

Both archetypes are found to be operative in the psyche of both sexes, but the archetypal feminine has always been more prominent in the female. Whether this is due to social conditioning or to genes has been a subject of debate. But what is a person, who is supposed to be the physical embodiment of an archetypal principle, expected to do when the society in which she lives does not recognize it as anything but an inferior function? She has only two possibilities.

On one hand she can repress the archetype within herself, like the male, and demand to participate as an equal (equally male, that is) among males. She can say that genital sexuality does not require her to live as an embodiment of the archetypal feminine. She can claim with good reason to be the equal of the male and live in the same world that he does. This would certainly solve the problem of woman's enslavement by man, but it would not solve the problem of the culture as a whole, the repression of one of the two fundamental archetypes. To say the least, woman is no better off repressing the archetypal feminine than man.

We are all embodiments of the two archetypes in varying mixtures, whether genitally male or female. Until we all learn to express both functions in our consciousness with ease, the repressed function will continue to be a source of difficulty both for individuals and the culture as a whole. Likewise, astrologers will not really be able to understand the Moon, except possibly insofar as the astrologer is liberated from the neurosis of the society. Therefore, the restitution of the feminine is the second route.

So the Moon represents the archetypal feminine, but how can we learn to understand it more fully? Ultimately some kind of psychotherapeutic process is necessary, but a beginning can be made by the study of mythology that comes from the period before the repression began.

In mythology we find not one, but several goddesses, each representing different aspects of the feminine. At the deepest level they always are associated with the Moon. By the same token we find more than one female planet in the heavens, but the Moon is the most fundamentally female of them all. She is the feminine in its deepest, most undifferentiated form, the Great Mother, the "eternal feminine," the Triple Goddess. It is especially this last aspect, the triple-faced goddess, that I wish to investigate in the remainder of this essay, for the feminine is not a static archetype but a changing one.

In his book *The Lunation Cycle*, Dane Rudhyar discusses the eight types of personality that come from the changing of the phases of the Moon. By contrast this will be a discussion of the change of the archetype in the phases of the Moon and the mythology that goes with it.

The goddess of the Moon usually is pictured in ancient mythology as possessing three faces (see Robert Graves, *The White Goddess*). The three faces correspond to the phases of the Moon. Why only three? Because the fourth face, that of the new Moon, is hidden in the glare of the Sun. The three faces of the goddess represent the transformation of the feminine archetype in the course of the month.

The first phase is the first-quarter Moon. This is the Moon as the maiden goddess of which Persephone-Proserpina is a good example, also Diana-Artemis, the maiden goddess of the hunt and the forest. The maiden goddess is the feminine first aware of her distinctness from the male. The Moon in the past week has just left the glare of the Sun and is now a celestial body perceived in her own right, not merely as a fugitive fleeing the Sun's rays.

The young girl is female, yet not ready for her encounter with the masculine principle. She is female, but not yet the full polar complement of the Sun. But she is the goddess of nascent life and as such is the goddess of spring, as in the case of Persephone. Also she is the goddess of Nature, far from the intrusions of the male principle, the secret creative processes of nature that go on in the wilds without the interference of men. The hunter who inadvertently gazed on Artemis bathing in the woods was turned into a stag and pursued to death by his own hunting dogs. This is the virgin phase of the goddess.

The next phase of the Moon is the full Moon. Now the feminine is ready for the confrontation with the masculine. She is now the goddess of fertility, of abundance. As Persephone was the maiden goddess, her mother, Ceres, is an example of the full-Moon type of goddess. As Diana and Artemis were maiden goddesses, Phoebe, the sister of the Sun god Apollo, is a full-Moon goddess.

Here the polar complementarity of the masculine and feminine archetypes is fully developed. At this stage in the cycle, the two are ready to play their roles as the father and mother of the universe, and on the earth plane, this symbolizes the period in the lives of both sexes where the sexual role is played. The feminine is now ready for and desirous of the encounter that the maiden goddess shunned. Here is Yin at its strongest. Mary, fruitful mother, yet eternal virgin. This is the mother protectress, protecting her young from the forces that they are not yet ready to encounter.

Yet the full Moon is usually considered to be a bad time. A full Moon in a horoscope is considered to be a difficult aspect to have. I think the reason for this has already been made clear in the preceding. If the feminine is at its height of power and influence in this phase and yet it is still repressed, it is most likely to cause the kind of trouble that repressed functions cause.

A personal comment may be of interest here. My own horoscope has Cancer rising with the Moon in close trine to the Ascendant. This gives the lunar archetype a rather strong power in my chart. Unlike many people I know, I find the time of the full Moon very peaceful and quieting and I rather enjoy sleeping in its light. Some people I have known are very edgy at the full-Moon time and cannot sleep.

If we were able to reestablish the archetypal feminine as a power in our souls and lives equal to that of the archetypal masculine, the full Moon might come to have a new significance. It would be a time of fruitfulness and creativity rather than of high crime rates and accidents.

Then comes the last quarter phase of the Moon. Here is the feminine past her peak of sexual creativity. This is the old woman, the wise woman. She is the elderly priestess who guards the gates of knowledge against the unwary intruder. Persephone as the wife of Hades, king of the underworld, is an example of this type of goddess. In fact, Persephone, the maiden, Ceres, the mother, and Persephone, the queen of the dead, are actually one goddess, the Triple Goddess. Likewise the Artemis-Phoebe pair is completed by the goddess Hecate, who rules all places where three roads come together, and guides the dead to the underworld. Another example is to be found in the three fates, Clotho, Lachesis and Atropos, who respectively spin, measure and cut the thread of life.

To the one who is ready to encounter the truths guarded by the old goddess, she is ready to aid and appears as the kindly old grandmother, the white witch. To one who is not, she is terrifying and threatening, the black witch. This is the aspect of the Moon goddess that is most often regarded as evil, but she is only evil to those who have not come to terms with the feminine archetype. She rules the doorway to the inner secrets of the psyche, just as the Sun rules the path to the truth of the outer world. Here is the source of the Moon's connection with the fourth house, which has a similar function among the houses.

The last phase is the invisible one, the new Moon. In the new Moon the masculine and feminine archetypes are in total union, undifferentiated oneness, the uroboros of self-begetting, God before the manifestation in twoness. It is interesting that the perfect conjunction of the Sun and Moon is a total eclipse of the Sun! In an eclipse both the Sun and Moon are blotted out for a moment and the whole world is plunged into a darkness that occurs at no other time. Those who have seen a total eclipse agree that it is one of the most unearthly experiences there is.

In the lunation the two archetypes are not united in sexual union as many seem to think. Sexual union requires an encounter between polar opposites. The new Moon is an obliteration of the polarity for the purpose of reformulating it anew. The myth symbol for this phase is the androgyne, with one-half male, one-half female features and body.

So here we have had an introduction to a new way of studying an archetype that we all experience but find very difficult to know at a conscious understanding level. Perhaps I have pointed the way to a new beginning of understanding symbolism in astrology.

2

The Wave Theory of Astrology

Several things have fallen into place, as they will magically from time to time in one's life, if you're a little bit lucky. One of them is that within twenty-four hours of listening to John Addey speak I had a chance to sit down and chat briefly with John Nelson, and he told me several things about his work in heliocentric astrology—all of which were very interesting but didn't make too much sense in terms of traditional astrology. And then John Addey spoke again, twenty-four hours later, and cleared up all the loopholes that John Nelson had left. So between the two of them something suddenly clicked, and basically what I am going to share with you is what clicked. This leaps off directly from where John Addey was working, and what I am basically going to do is propose a model of how astrology works, and describe some of the consequences on a practical level. This will, of course, be difficult to accomplish. All I can do is give a sketch of the basic principles.

First of all, what are astrological influences, what do they actually contain? There have been many explanations, and I don't propose that this is in any way, shape, or form a final explanation, but it behaves very nicely. One of the oldest explanations is that the planets were gods, and of course being gods they had this effect. This is not a fashionable theory today, so we'll drop that one immediately. More recently, in the nineteenth century, when radio waves and things like this were discovered, astrologers started talking about vibrations. That is to say, it was as if the planets were sending out electromagnetic waves that somehow or other made up the qualities of the planet. Saturn was turning out a Saturn sort of magnetic wave, Jupiter was turning out a Jupiter sort of magnetic wave. And when you read people like Alan Leo and a lot of the old nineteenth-century astrologers, they talk about benefic versus malefic rays, afflicted rays, adverse rays, and the whole thing begins to take on a very pseudo-scientific overtone. This is not meant to ridicule those theories, but they weren't really scientific models, because the astrologers were taking only the language, and none of the mathematical components.

More recently Jung proposed the theory of synchronicity, which is basically that the planets don't cause anything but simply are somehow correlated with events on Earth from the very beginning of time. There is somehow a repeated cyclical pattern throughout the universe. It is found in human events, terrestrial events, meteorology, the stock-market rhythms and the planets. Now, the planets are the only one of these that is mathematically forecastable, so consequently we look at the planets to find out what the, shall we say, underlying rhythms of life are.

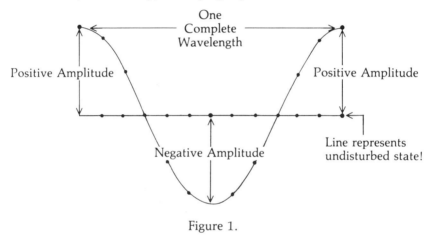

Figure 1.

Then John Addey did his work in which he discovered that there were phenomena in astrology that acted very much like waves with harmonics, overtone series and a whole lot of things like that. Figure 1 will help you to visualize this concept. You can start a wave at any point—I chose to start it at the top because this is the way I believe the aspect waves work. The line represents an undisturbed state, or the way things would be naturally. A wave starts at a certain height above the line; that point is called its amplitude. The wave then declines, crosses the undisturbed or normal line and reaches a minimum amplitude, which is exactly the same as the high amplitude. Then it goes back up again and continues this pattern. These waves are generated by the trigonometric function of sine and cosine, and are consequently called sine waves. If you don't know any trigonometry, suffice it to say that if you find the sine or cosine of any number and you keep on plotting it on the graph, you get something that goes on ad infinitum. As children, you've probably taken a clothes line and plucked it and then watched the undulation of the clothes line—that's a sine wave. In fact, that's one of the first times I ever saw one, doing that very thing.

Now, another quality of the sine wave with which we should be familiar is the wavelength, which is the distance between two corresponding components of two waves, between two peaks or two bottoms. Now, waves travel in straight lines. A certain number of waves will pass a given point in a second, and that is called the frequency of the wave—the number of waves you have per second. Waves are measured in cycles per second, and the calculations are called "hertz" in honor of the man who discovered electromagnetic waves, a German named Heinrich Hertz.

Now, the harmonic of a wave simply refers to the fact that waves are not usually pure. Most often you find small waves on top of large waves, and the small waves have a smaller amplitude than the larger waves, but they are always some even division of the bigger wave. Usually the most common ones that you encounter are twice the size of the large wave, three times the large wave, four times the large wave, five times, etc., and as the number gets higher the wave gets smaller and gradually trails off into nothingness. These are called harmonics or overtones and they invariably are present in any given type of wave. A flute, for example, creates a musical wave that has almost no overtones at all, and if you hear a musical tone generated by a laboratory frequency generator, it sounds very much like a flute, a pure sine wave tone. But, if you start adding harmonics it starts changing the effect of the tone. What it does primarily is to put an edge on it. An oboe or a violin have musical tones with an "edge" on them; they are not "round" like the tone of a flute. And this is because both the oboe and the violin are very rich in high harmonics, and that gives them a penetrating, sharp-edge quality.

Typical of one of John Addey's discoveries was his investigation, for example, of the distribution around the zodiac of the natal Suns of doctors. He found, as most students of the subject have found, that there is very little correlation between Sun signs and the birthdays of doctors. What he did find, however, was that doctors tend to be born at 72-degree intervals through the zodiac, one-fifth of the circle. Treating the year as a fundamental tone, as a sine wave, he found that there was a very strong fifth harmonic in the distribution of the Suns of doctors. This is rather fascinating considering that there is a traditional association between the number five and the art of healing, as suggested by the ancient numerologists who knew nothing about waves, harmonics, vibrations or anything else. There is also a work by Johann Kepler called the *World Harmonies* in which he discusses analogies between astrological phenomena and musical tones. For example: the fundamental tone or note of an astrological rhythm is the time between two successive conjunctions. Take the month. From new moon to new moon is the fundamental cycle of the month. The first harmonic of that is from new moon to full moon to new moon, that is, one half of a month, and that corresponds to what we call the opposition. Then the fourth harmonic is from new moon to first quarter to full moon to third quarter to new moon, going around in fourths. That corresponds astrologically to what we call the square. And the trine corresponds to the third harmonic, from conjunction to waxing trine to waning trine to conjunction. And so forth: all of the astrological aspects can be related to harmonics of waves.

Now, very much implicit in John Addey's work is that what we are dealing with is somehow or other the harmonics of these cycles. These are called synodic cycles. A synod is a conjunction. It simply means a coming together of two things. This raises a few problems. First of all, if the synodic cycle is a wave, it is a wave of exceedingly low energy. This is because the longer the wavelength of a wave, the lower its energy content. I don't know the exact formula, but it is an inverse relationship. If a wave is very short it has a very high amount of energy per wave. Light has a certain amount of energy, infra-red a lesser amount, radio waves lesser yet, and the longest waves we have been able to detect have wavelengths of several miles. Though they are still thousands of cycles per second, they are extremely low in energy. You can imagine what happens when we get down to a cycle that is one cycle every 492 years, what its energy content would be—almost nothing. So, immediately it becomes evident that this cannot be quite the relationship we want.

At this point I have to introduce another basic distinction in types of waves. There are two kinds of waves: those that move, called traveling waves, and standing waves, which do not move in space.

In his lectures, John Addey used a demonstration with magnets that filled in the missing piece. It isn't the synodic rhythms that are causing harmonics, rather it's something quite different.

This was his theory about what the trine represented (see figure 2). These two circles here represent planets in trine. The circle across the middle at the center is the Earth, and the arrows simply are pointing at the two planets. What Addey said was that it seemed as if the position of the planets created a kind of positive field. A third positive field completed the grand trine, and negative fields were located approximately where the sextiles would be located.

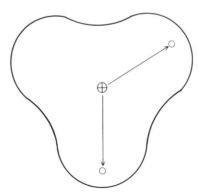

Figure 2. Third-Harmonic Wave in Circle. No Overtones

What he drew was a picture of a standing wave in a circle. This wave isn't going anywhere. What came to mind is that the zodiac or ecliptic is like a guitar string, only it's circular instead of linear. Now, some very funny things happen to guitar strings. If you pluck a guitar string, you primarily get the fundamental pitch, but if you listen carefully you can hear other notes going, too: those are the harmonics. If you put your finger half way down the guitar string, and touch it lightly exactly half way and pluck it, you get the octave of that tone without any of the fundamental at all. This is because by putting your finger in the middle you remove the fundamental and leave only the harmonics. That is an example of a harmonic standing wave.

My basic proposition is simply this: the planets are like the fingers. The zodiac is in a continual state of ringing, but it is full of many different basic waves, making absolutely no sense or order whatsoever—what we would call in physics white noise—a mixture of all frequencies with no particular bias toward any frequency. What the planets do as they go around the zodiac is form angles, which represent even whole-number subdivisions of a circle. They stop out all those vibrations that will not fit in between them. So, when two planets are 120 degrees apart they will remove from this white-noise configuration all vibrations that will not divide evenly into 120 degrees. This includes the conjunction and the opposition. As you will see shortly, it does not include, oddly enough, the square.

As this goes on, you will not only have a wave of 120 degrees, but you also get wave lengths of 60 degrees, 30 degrees, 15 degrees, 7½ degrees, and so forth, because these all divide evenly into 120 degrees. These all have a curious quality. If the 120-degree wave were a musical tone, the 60-degree wave would be an octave above it, the 30-degree wave would be an octave above that, the 15 would be another octave, and the 7½ would be another octave—in other words, 7½, 15, 30, 60 and 120 are all the same tone. We know that the trine and the sextile are very similar in nature. The basic difference seems to be that the sextile is not quite as strong as the trine. And of course, in traditional astrology there are other distinctions based on the fact that the sextile is a third- or an eleventh-house aspect, the trine is a fifth- or ninth-house aspect. This, I suggest, has nothing whatsoever to do with the aspect, but only with the fact that it falls into houses in certain ways. Basically, this suggests that the sextile is nothing but the octave of the trine, and therefore that they would be fundamentally similar in nature. If the trine were the note A, the sextile would be the A an octave above that. Similarly, if we take the fundamental, which is the conjunction, its octave will be the opposition, the double octave will be the square, the triple octave will be the 45 and the 135, and the fourth octave will be the 22½. The Germans and particularly the Uranians and Cosmobiologists have experimented with these. And as some of you may know, we are also going to the 11¼ and halves of that. So again, these aspects, which traditionally have been considered to be rather similar, turn out to be, in terms of this theory, octaves of each other. There will also be differences between them, however, because there are many factors involved here.

So, John Addey pointed out something rather important when he showed us that the trine wave in figure 2 does not correspond very well to what we know to be the behavior of a trine. For one thing, you will notice that this trine has an orb of plus or minus 30 degrees. There aren't too many astrologers, even among the most traditionally oriented, who will allow an orb that large, because it carries all the way from the trine to the square, and to define a square as being at the end of the orb of the trine is a little strange. Similarly, if we did a fourth-harmonic wave here, the square would have an orb of about plus or minus 22½ degrees. But then Addey went on to point out something else, and this was the clincher of the whole model. If you take a wave and superimpose its various octaves on it, you create the effect of sharpening the peak tremendously. The peak increases in amplitude: that is to say, instead of remaining quite low, it goes much higher, and instead of being wide and graceful, it becomes almost a point, like a peak. What this suggests is that the aspect is the sum total of the fundamental and all of its octaves put together. How many octaves we don't really know, but probably quite a few.

What happens is illustrated by the first of two graphs (see figure 3), the Third Harmonic Wave and Five Octave Waves (6, 12, 24, 48, 96). This is what I decided to do. There is obviously a direct relationship between the amplitude of the harmonic, that is, how widely it swings around the fundamental, and the tightness of the peaks. So I asked several physicists what it is in a musical tone that determines the quantity of harmonics in the fundamental wave. Well, you can answer what it is in a musical tone—it has something to do with the shape of the cavity in which the sound is taking place, and something to do with the medium that is vibrating around it. That is, if you have a guitar, the shape of the guitar body, the thickness of the wood, and the shape of the cavity inside the body all have the effect of reinforcing certain harmonics and de-emphasizing others. But the question I asked was: suppose you had an ideal medium where there was no inherent entity to reinforce any wave at the expense of any other wave? The answer I got was that there really is no such thing as a postulated ideal resonant medium. So, rather than say we have raised a new issue in science here, let me just say that nobody I know has been able to answer the question.

What I did was to figure out a very simple way of adding together a fundamental and its overtones. It's very simple mathematically. But because of what it involved, doing it was another matter. I don't know if any of you have ever had any trigonometry, but all I would have had to do is to look at the one-degree intervals, the cosine of a number, the cosine of twice that number, the cosine of four times, eight times, sixteen times, and thirty-two and add them together. That would have taken approximately five minutes per calculation. I had 120 of them and I'm not that patient. So, being a dedicated fanatic, I went deeply into the red. [This was written in 1974, before microcomputers, but I found a machine that did it for me automatically.] And the first thing I ran off on the machine was this model, and these are the results I got. I decided, more or less arbitrarily, that the ideal resonant medium would have the effect of making no distinction whatever between the various harmonics, and there is no reason to assume actually that there is in fact any variation whatsoever in the amplitude of the harmonics. The model I am presenting to you is a model in which all the harmonics have the same amplitude. This does not mean that a 30-degree angle is as intense as a trine. Although the 30-degree angle has in it the 30, the 15, and the 7½, the 120 has in it the 120, the 60, the 30, the 15 and the 7½. So, automatically, the trine will have a vastly greater intensity than any of its octaves, because it has all of the octaves plus itself. Figure 3 is the result of this, and figure 4, labeled Values of the Third Harmonic by Degrees, is a collection of the numbers corresponding to the graph. If I assign an amplitude of one to all of the cosine waves of the harmonics, then the trine comes out having a value of plus 6. If we move to a one-degree orb out of trine we get 4.45. One degree and you notice a considerable drop. Two degrees and it's down to 2½. At 3 degrees it rises up slightly because of one of the lower harmonics beginning to rise—2.56. Then it drops down radically at 5 to 0.83, hangs in there and then at 7 it rises up again. What's that? That's the 7½ degree wave that Edith Wangemann, in Germany, has discovered to be extremely powerful in her delineations.

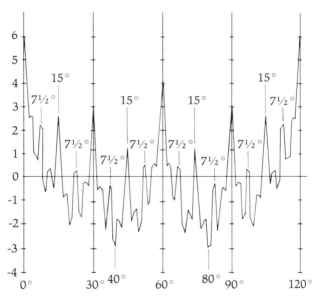

Figure 3. Third-Harmonic Wave and Five Octave Waves (6, 12, 24, 48, 96)

And what we have here seems to be a mathematical verification of that. I submit that if the amplitude of these waves were anything less than one each, the 7½-degree wave would be absolutely experientially undetectable. However, it is not undetectable in experience: it seems to be quite powerful. I have determined that there are fundamentally different kinds of personality types associated with people who have large numbers of 7½- or 11¼-degree multiples (11¼ comes from successively dividing the square by 2). And that, just as in the musical tone in which high harmonics give a sort of sharp incisive edge to the note, high harmonics in astrology seem to do the same thing to a personality.

0	6.00	31	1.41	62	0.48	93	-0.18
1	4.45	32	-0.58	63	0.58	94	-0.21
2	2.47	33	-0.49	64	0.44	95	-1.61
3	2.56	34	-0.62	65	-1.10	96	-1.50
4	2.39	35	-2.12	66	-1.14	97	0.32
5	0.83	36	-2.12	67	0.52	98	0.24
6	0.76	37	-0.39	68	0.26	99	-1.75
7	2.39	38	-0.58	69	-1.92	100	-2.00
8	2.08	39	-2.66	70	-2.37	101	-0.70
9	-0.14	40	-3.00	71	-1.27	102	-0.72
10	-0.63	41	-1.79	72	-1.50	103	-0.91
11	0.40	42	-1.90	73	-1.90	104	1.07
12	0.12	43	-2.16	74	-0.14	105	2.71
13	-0.34	44	-0.27	75	1.29	106	1.35
14	1.34	45	1.29	76	-0.27	107	-0.34
15	2.71	46	-0.14	77	-2.16	108	0.12
16	1.06	47	-1.90	78	-1.90	109	0.41
17	-0.91	48	-1.50	79	-1.79	110	-0.63
18	-0.72	49	-1.27	80	-3.00	111	-0.14
19	-0.70	50	-2.36	81	-2.66	112	2.08
20	-2.00	51	-1.92	82	-0.58	113	2.39
21	-1.75	52	0.26	83	-0.39	114	0.76
22	0.24	53	0.52	84	-2.12	115	0.83
23	0.32	54	-1.14	85	-2.12	116	2.39
24	-1.50	55	-1.10	86	-0.62	117	2.56
25	-1.61	56	0.44	87	-0.49	118	2.47
26	-0.21	57	0.58	88	-0.58	119	4.45
27	-0.18	58	0.48	89	1.41	120	6.00
28	-0.37	59	2.45	90	3.00		
29	1.51	60	4.00	91	1.51		
30	3.00	61	2.45	92	-0.37		

Figure 4. Values of the Third Harmonic by Degrees

Most of you don't know me too well, but my chart is a great mass of trines. I am not a particularly trinal personality, but when you look at my chart, on a 90-degree dial, you see that it is a string of 11¼'s, which are derived from squares and oppositions. And if I were to add the amplitudes of all the 11¼-degree waves that are together in my chart, it probably would come out to several squares. I have similarly found other people with lots of squares in which the 7½ degrees were strong. There was a strong trinal influence in their personality that was not detectable in terms of gross aspects.

We continue on, and after 8 degrees it drops down to the negative, and it continues falling until it reaches 20 degrees where it's −2. And then it goes up again to +3 at 30, which is the double octave of the trine, and then falls to its all-time low at 40, which is negative 3.

Question: "How do you account for this—the statement you made just a minute ago indicating in your specific case a lot of 11¼'s coming up which are multiples or subharmonics of the square aspect—is this a possible overlapping of the trine and the square?"

No, what happens is that between the planets that are not in traditional aspect are aspects that are 11¼-degree multiples, and there are a lot more of those than there are of anything else. As a matter of fact, on the 90-degree dial my chart ties into one enormous string of 11¼'s, which includes, either by midpoints or directly, everything in my chart. My chart is basically one 11¼-degree mess, which is fine with me, because if I had nothing but trines, I think I would probably be a vegetable. My experience with overdoses of trines is that they indicate that sort of personality—very happy—but it's sort of an astrological prefrontal lobotomy to have that many trines. I must except, however, the grand trine, because for those of you who are into planetary pictures, the grand trine is three rather horrendous planetary pictures, three oppositions. So the grand trine does not have quite the same effect as a simple trine.

Now, something very strange happens here if you look at figure 3. I'd like to call your attention to some of the rather curious factors. At 90 degrees it's at +3 again. And why? Because 90 degrees is three double octaves of a trine. It's three-quarters of a trine. So the trine wave does include the square. But now if we go to figure 5, which shows the first harmonic by 3-degree intervals (same set of numbers, but it goes by 3 degrees instead of one) you will discover that the fundamental conjunction wave does not include the trine. Notice that at 120 degrees, we are at a bottom rather than a peak, and in general the third harmonic of any series does not fit into the fundamental, or the octaves; it is always at the most negative point. This suggests something we already know—that the fundamental and the third harmonic of the conjunction and the trine are radically different in nature.

The strange thing about this model is that it shows many things that we know to be true. It also shows a few things that although we didn't really know, John Addey suspected. If you look at the intensity of the trine again, you will see that it does not, as Donald Bradley thought, decrease as a sine wave, but it goes down like this. A trine that is 5 degrees out of orb has less intensity than a trine that is 7½ degrees out of orb. And this ties in very well with Edith Wangemann's discovery that 127½ degrees is trine-like in nature, but is not exactly a trine. There is something else going on there. It is a trine of +7½. This model seems to suggest that this would be the case. If you look at the graphic representation of the third harmonic, you will see that it has peaks every 7½ degrees. Now you will notice that all 7½-degree aspects are not created equal. They are all peaks relative to the degrees around them, but some of them are higher than others. The ones nearest to the trine are the highest. They are almost as high as the 15 and the 30. Between the 15 and the 30 the 7½-degree peak is just barely positive. The one between 30 and 45 is negative. This is probably what gives rise to the fact that there is a difference between the various multiples of any given number. For example the second sextile, which is 1/12, does not have the same quality as the quincunx, which is 5/12. And again, the various heights of this curve suggest that the various repetitions of the harmonics would not have the same quality. Another thing it shows you is that the orbs of even a trine are rather small. Well, it depends on what you want to take as an orb. All I can say is that the intensity level has decreased dramatically in 5 degrees, and it decreases most dramatically between 4 and 5 degrees, where it suddenly drops about two points.

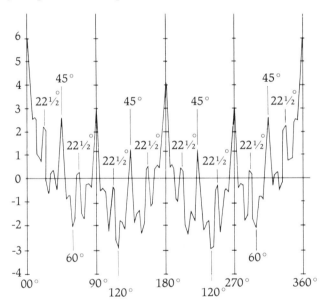

Figure 5. First-Harmonic Wave and Five Octave Waves (2, 4, 8, 16, 32)

As I listened to Mike Munkasey [the previous lecturer that day], I immediately wanted to try using what he described instead of the sine wave as curves of aspects. We might find something rather striking happening when we do. Now the gross assumption I have made here, the one which vitiates—well, it doesn't vitiate the essence of the idea, but does vitiate these graphs to some extent—is the assumption that all the harmonics have the same basic amplitude. That may or may not be true, and that I'm afraid is what is called in science an experimental question. One thing we have to figure out is some way of testing this model. This model predicts many things we know to be true, but it also says some things that we haven't before realized, like the fact that aspects do not decay in intensity at a constant downhill rate as the orb increases. Rather they decay erratically as the orb increases. That's something rather new.

Question: "Is there any reason why you stopped at 32?"

Yes, my computer would run out of gas if I went further. As a matter of fact, this obviously would have to decay to infinity, but somewhere along the line, I suspect, there is an amplitude dropoff. Although we have Theodor Landscheidt in Germany discoursing about the 1028th harmonic, he is either wrong, or the 1028th harmonic is detectable. At this point we are left in the position where only the technologists will be able to help us. This can't be done with my crude, simple, basic techniques—dials and things like that.

Now, radio waves that we receive in our AM squawk box, with all its static and the idiotic DJ's and so forth, are amplitude-modulated waves (that's what AM means). That means the amplitude of the signal of the radio station varies in a way that enables the radio to deduce from that wave the sounds that the announcer spoke into the microphone at the studio. A radio is basically a logically deductive device for picking up information out of radio signals. That's not the way it is usually considered, but it is one way of approaching it. I submit that the human brain is very much the same kind of apparatus, only the signals in this case are the standing waves generated by the planets in the zodiac. And basically, we have that information carried by the fundamental, by its octave, by its third, fourth, fifth, and so forth down the line, harmonics. Except for one thing: the second and fourth are octaves of each other and will convey essentially the same information. Similarly, the third and sixth. So what we are really left with is the prime numbers only. One is not technically a prime number, but we'll include it with 2, 3, 5, 7, 11 and so forth. Each of these harmonics of the fundamental conveys information, and treating the solar system as being a meta-programming device, each conveys information that varies in nature according to the number of the harmonic. We count only the prime-number harmonics, because any even number will simply be the octave of a prime number. This in turn is modified by the planets that are making up the wave. The wave is obviously not independent of the planets. We have two basic components: The wave function created by the angle between the planets, and somehow or other the planets contributing a unique quality of their own.

I do not have any idea how they do this. This may be where the synodic rhythm comes in somehow. It may be that the length of the synodic cycle of two planets determines the quality of the relationship between those planets. The aspect itself is not a harmonic of the synodic cycle, but rather is created by these zodiacal standing waves, which could have an intensity considerably greater than the energy content of the synodic cycles.

What we are basically doing is picking up a kind of radio signal and each pair of planets is transmitting data to us on one of these waves except when the planets are separated by an angle that is incommensurable with the circle. That is to say, when the ratio between the angle and 360 degrees is an irrational number, one that cannot be expressed as a fraction of any sort whatsoever. Then you have a total disconnection between the two planets. And this would happen at intervals through the synodic cycle of two planets. There would be periods in which their angular separation had no relationship whatsoever to the circle, and during those times the two planets would be absolutely disconnected. This could give us a kind of negative aspect, which I will christen, for lack of a better name, the disjunction or total lack of connection by aspect. The only thing is that these would have to be extremely precise to be of any value at all—within seconds, not minutes, because it is the nature of an irrational number to be surrounded by points that are rational. But I suspect that you could have a small error of a few seconds and still have it go in. So this model generates the possibility of a whole new kind of angular relationship—the disjunction, indicating two planets that are totally non-integrated with each other, in no way, shape, or form, and at no level of intensity.

A second thing it suggests is what John Nelson discovered. John Nelson was a radio propagation analyst for RCA. His job was to find a means of forecasting those times when the earth's ionosphere would be so disturbed that radio signals wouldn't bounce off it, and transatlantic radio transmission would be interfered with, because the signals would go off into space and that would be the end of them. He discovered that these disturbances occur in what we astrologically call the hard aspects: 0, 90, 180, and to a lesser extent 45 and 135. He discovered that the periods of unusually clear transmission coincided with what we call the good aspects: 60 and 120. This again shows the dramatically opposite nature of the third harmonic and the first harmonic. Please also note that the conjunction behaves like a hard aspect, it does not behave like a trine, even though it is, in a way, part of a trine series. You know, 0, 120, 240, 0—around the circle like that. The conjunction was of a hard nature. Nelson discovered several situations in which the intensity of a storm was totally disconnected from the number and strength of the aspects involved. He would find one little square and everything would just go absolutely crazy. Well, when he began analyzing this, he discovered that the square had one of these little micro-aspects—particularly the 11¼ or 7½—aspecting it with a high degree of precision at exactly its moment of perfection. What that did, according to this model, was to set up a second standing wave with a smaller wavelength that was exactly in phase with the first standing wave. This would cause the peaks to go up tremendously, to decrease more sharply and to generally increase the amplitude of the stress. Nelson also discovered that if he had a whole string of these little aspects with no big aspects, the ionosphere would go crazy.

But, one thing had to be the case—all the 7½'s had to be in 7½-degree multiples of each other. That is, they had to all form at once. If you had a situation like this, with a 7½ here and another over here, and this between them, not a multiple of 7½, then nothing would happen. This suggests that the effect of these two 7½'s is to cancel each other out since they are not tied in with each other. This correlates with my experience in my professional work, which is that the 7½- and 11¼-degree multiples must be all tied together in one string or nothing happens, and this fits very well with the idea that when you add them all together you get a gigantic amplitude composed of lots of tiny little aspects. You just add them together arithmetically, the amplitude of that to the amplitude of this, etc.

Question: "Conceivably then we could develop from this model the idea of a person's chart in terms of wave amplitude and frequency."

Exactly. Mainly what it can do is to give us a rigorous version of Marc Edmund Jones' basic temperamental types. Because you'll notice that some of Jones' types—you look at them and they just don't seem to be quite there. What you could do is make a circular plot, and you might find that there were quantities going in various directions in the chart that represented high intensity areas and others that represented low intensity areas. I haven't quite figured out how to work this out yet, but it somehow logically follows, and we might be able to get a basic classification of astrological types based on these kinds of distributions. Fortunately, this is not hard. It's hard to do with ordinary methods, but, using the machine, I generated figure 6 in approximately twenty minutes. The machine is expensive, but it is not out of everyone's reach.

Question: "I can give you a good practical working example of the harmonic use in the horoscope. I analyzed all the harmonics that exist in the sextile in my particular horoscope, and of all the sextiles there, all the sextiles worked out with two or three connections to harmonics with the exception of one sextile, which worked out with nine major connections. And I said, 'My goodness, why is it that all of a sudden this one sextile could have all these connections.' And of course when I got to looking at my chart, it had to be the one sextile that stands out in my chart. So, it was just another confirmation of a very important point in the chart."

Right, one thing I should point out here, I believe it will be necessary to analyze the horoscope at each harmonic level. You should not combine anything on one harmonic level but the octaves, because the third harmonics of any wave represent a different signal, they are different qualities. Of course the Hindus have done this with their harmonic horoscopes. They primarily stress the octave harmonics, although they do use trines and sextiles in them too. But I think they're mucking things up. What you would have to do is examine independently each horoscope at the first, second, third, fifth, seventh, eleventh, and so forth, harmonic level.

From a practical point of view I wouldn't carry it much beyond nine, because you would have to detect it at the rather gross levels before worrying about incredible refinements. This is why I am a little disturbed at Landscheidt and his 1028th harmonic. We've got other fish to fry first, like how about the ninth harmonic. How many people use 40-degree multiple aspects? That's the ninth harmonic, or nonile, which is another name for it. And there is a binonile, a seminonile and so forth. And God knows what they mean. All we know about is the information-carrying qualities of the first, second, third, fourth, eighth, twelfth and sixth. Those are really the only ones we know how to use. We know a little bit about the fifth, we know nothing about the seventh, ninth and eleventh.

0	6.00	93	1.41	186	0.48	279	-0.18
3	4.45	96	-0.58	189	0.58	282	-0.21
6	2.47	99	-0.49	192	0.43	285	-1.61
9	2.56	102	-0.62	195	-1.10	288	-1.50
12	2.39	105	-2.12	198	-1.14	291	0.32
15	0.83	108	-2.12	201	0.52	294	0.24
18	0.76	111	-0.39	204	0.26	297	-1.75
21	2.39	114	-0.58	207	-1.92	300	-2.00
24	2.08	117	-2.66	210	-2.37	303	-0.70
27	-0.14	120	-3.00	213	-1.27	306	-0.72
30	-0.63	123	-1.79	216	-1.50	309	-0.90
33	0.40	126	-1.90	219	-1.89	312	-1.06
36	0.12	129	-2.16	222	-0.14	315	2.71
39	-0.34	132	-0.27	225	1.29	318	1.35
42	1.35	135	1.29	228	-0.27	321	-0.34
45	2.71	138	-0.14	231	-2.16	324	0.12
48	1.06	141	-1.89	234	-1.90	327	0.41
51	-0.91	144	-1.50	237	-1.79	330	-0.63
54	-0.72	147	-1.27	240	-3.00	333	-0.14
57	-0.70	150	-2.37	243	-2.66	336	2.08
60	-2.00	153	-1.92	247	-0.58	339	2.36
63	-1.75	156	0.26	249	-0.39	342	0.76
66	0.24	159	0.52	252	-2.12	345	0.83
69	0.32	162	1.14	255	-2.12	348	2.39
72	-1.50	165	-1.10	258	-0.62	351	2.56
75	-1.61	168	0.44	261	-0.49	354	2.47
78	-0.21	171	0.58	264	-0.58	357	4.45
81	-0.18	174	0.48	267	1.41	360	6.00
84	-0.37	177	2.45	270	3.00		
87	1.51	180	4.00	273	1.51		
90	3.00	183	2.45	276	-0.37		

Figure 6. Values of the First Harmonic by Three-Degree Intervals

I know there are a lot of things I haven't been able to cover. There are a lot of loose ends, but I hope something came through.

3

Mercury, the Modulator

It is necessary at times to open oneself to the universal flows of energy that manifest themselves as astrological symbols, and to inquire with both soul and intellect as to their true inner and essential meanings. Astrological delineations tend to concern themselves with superficials, with external manifestations rather than deep, inner essential cores of meaning. There are at least two principal reasons for this.

The first reason is that the day-to-day practical concerns of the working astrologer do not lend themselves to abstract speculation. Trying to deal with the problems of a client's "love, luck and money," which is still demanded of the astrologer, tends to trivialize the astrologer's mind. This is compounded by the fact that, until fairly recently, astrology was too "far out" to attract the best minds of the era—minds capable of dealing with the kind of abstract issues that are necessary to keep astrological symbolism intellectually alive. Consequently, the symbolism has suffered.

Two kinds of research, therefore, will be necessary to further the evolution of astrology: scientific on one hand, humanistic and symbolic on the other. This paper deals with the latter and is an inquiry into the nature of the planet Mercury. Of necessity, it is somewhat limited. More research into the nature of the symbol Mercury is definitely desirable, but in this paper I have laid down a few basic principles I hope will help release the symbol and make it live again in our consciousness.

Mercury as a planetary symbol has not struck me as one of the most gripping. Astrologers tend to pass lightly over it in favor of discussing more dramatic symbols such as Mars, Venus or Saturn. When the effects of these are confronted, it is usually a moving, dramatic experience that leaves little untouched. It is, therefore, not difficult to associate these planets with visceral feelings as well as intellectual understanding. I do not believe, however, this is the case with the symbolism of Mercury, at least not as it is normally understood.

As usually understood by astrologers, Mercury is pictured as a beardless youth—young to the point of being asexual, with a not very muscular build, with winged feet and holding a curious staff with two intertwined serpents whose obvious occult significance contrasts oddly with the rest of the picture. We have here a celestial Western Union boy, a messenger of the gods, a figure with about as much psychic impact as his modern counterpart. The other planets still impress us as "godlike," but with Mercury there is little of the numinous aura we associate with godhood.

Mercury rules speed, communication, transportation, thought, intellect, the nerves, the wind, the breath, the lungs and, because of his youth, young people of both sexes. All of this is clear enough but devoid of major psychic impact. Of course, since according to traditional astrology Mercury rules the dry, unimpassioned intellect, we should not expect emotional involvement in its symbolism. Still, I feel there is far more to it than that. Other Mercury symbols have not been as dry as ours has become. For example, there is the German Mercury, Wotan, who gave one of his eyes that he might possess perfect knowledge and travel about in a thundercloud. Also, there is the rather strange figure of Hermes Trismegistus, the mythical founder of alchemy. These figures lead me to believe that Mercury, more than other symbols, has been a victim of the trivializing process described above, and that serious study and reflection are necessary to revive it.

Astrology consists of a very primitive, yet profoundly wise mythical symbolism—primitive in that it represents a kind of thinking which precedes logical, rational thought; and wise in that it embodies concepts and understandings that cannot be conveyed any other way, and may be, in many respects, superior to rational, logical thought. For the symbols to continue to convey essential meanings to us, we must make an effort to understand them and perceive them in our daily lives. Otherwise they die or, rather, our ability to comprehend their truth dies. This is how religions die: the dogmas become fixed, and formulated creed replaces living experience. The near-death of astrology in the seventeenth century was due to this. The underlying metaphysical philosophy of astrology died, and only the outer fortune-telling husk survived. Toonder and West in their book *The Case for Astrology* make this point very strongly.

Mercury, or Mercurius as he is called by the ancients, was believed by them to be identical with the Greek Hermes and the Egyptian Thoth. It can be seen from the first quotation from the Memphite theology of ancient Egypt that the symbol of Mercury-Hermes-Thoth was considered a good deal more profound by the ancients than it is by us. He is the enunciator of the Divine Will, the one who puts the primal urge to manifest into concrete being. To give him a designation in terms of Christian tradition, he is the Logos principle.

According to ancient myths, and spiritual and mystical teachings ever since, the universe is a cosmic living One. (See Dane Rudhyar's *The Planetarization of Consciousness.*) There is the One and only the One. Nothing can be conceived of outside of it. There is only the Oneself. But the One alternately creates and destroys a universe (uni-versus, literally the One turning) within itself as a result of its desires to reflect upon itself and to experience its own existence. Because there is nothing external to itself wherein it can reflect its own existence, it must divide itself. It must create a fictitious subject to do the experiencing and a fictitious object to be experienced. We do much the same thing whenever we self-reflect. We say, "*I* reflect upon *myself*." "I" and "myself" are fictitious, for there is still only the one person self-reflecting.

So the One divided itself into a Self aspect and an Unself aspect. The Self aspect is that part of the universe that sees the other half, the Unself aspect. The Self is psyche, and all consciousness of whatever form or level, and it permeates all matter and energy. The Unself aspect of the One manifests itself as the physical universe, which is the object of our perception and in which our civilization is so utterly wrapped up. In all of this there is still only the One reflecting upon itself and experiencing all possible experience within itself. Eventually, in each cycle of manifestation, all possible experience is experienced by the One, all consciousness (Self, subject) realizes that it is one with itself and all the physical universe (Unself, object) and the cycle of manifestation ends in a gigantic mystical experience.

Between the creation and the mystical death of the universe, another principle must be operative—a principle that connects the manifestations of the Divine Will to the original wellsprings of the Divine Will deep within the unmanifest base of the universe.

In the Memphite theology of ancient Egypt, creation is achieved because a divine principle comes into existence that formulates the impulses of the cosmic Self into words and thoughts, which thereby become created beings. This is Thoth, our Mercury, playing a role somewhat more vital than we usually give him. The universal One split into Self and Unself aspects gives rise to an energy flow that transmits its intents throughout the psychic and physical halves of the universe. This flow achieves exactly the same purpose for the universe as the nerves of our body do for the physical body and, of course, the nerves are ruled by Mercury in astrology. There is always to be found an information-carrying flow between all aspects of creation and the fundamental ground of the universe. It connects all psychic contents to the Self aspect of the One and all physical creation to the Unself aspect of the One. All manifestation, either psychic or physical, is connected to the One by this same logos power of Thoth-Hermes-Mercury. Thought, in the broadest sense of the term, and physical manifestation are simply two different manifestations of the same energy. Through "thought" all forms of psychic activity must be understood, not simply "thought" in the narrow, linear, logical sense of the term traditionally symbolized by Mercury. This lower-level identification of Mercury has come about because our civilization has ceased to recognize the validity of the other types of thought.

At the same time, Mercury is not quite thought itself, nor is it physical law. It is the ordering principle which translates Divine Will into the twin manifestations of being, psyche and physis. Perhaps it now may be made clear why Mercury rules the dual sign Gemini. The symbol for Gemini, it is believed by many students, has nothing to do with Castor and Pollux. It is actually the two columns of Isis representing the twin halves of the universe, the unmanifest, internal, or hidden (psyche) and the manifest (physis). Thoth is not the word itself, but the creator-formulator and transmitter of the word.

Thoth-Hermes-Mercury precedes the division of the world into the primal duality of Self and Unself from which all other duality derives. Therefore he has none of the characteristics that we associate with duality—hence his sexlessness. Everything he does, however, is translated into both realms. In an alchemical treatise, he is described as both father and mother, good and evil, male and female, high and low, etc.

"I am known and yet do not exist at all." Mercury is part of all existence in that he formulates the Divine Will, yet is prior to all of its manifestations by which we know the universe. Mercury defies all categories because all of our categories have their origin in the primal duality, which he precedes. He is amoral because he precedes morality; asexual because he precedes sex. He is young, but he is also very old in alchemical literature. There is a very strong tie-in between Mercury and Saturn in alchemy, which astrology has somehow lost track of. Both youth and old age are androgynous periods in life because of their closeness to birth and death, the paths into and out of manifestation. Hermes conveyed souls to the underworld in ancient Greece.

Alchemists sought the divine Mercury that was in every substance. They sought not the chemical substance, as does the modern chemist, but the divine principle of which the substance was a manifestation. Direct apprehension of the Mercurial principle would bring one to an understanding of the Primal One. To put the same thing into contemporary mystical language, it would bring them to enlightenment. Enlightenment was the "alchemical gold," the path back to Horus, the heart, the Sun, the Primal One. Actual material gold was not the goal at all. This is largely a popular view based on a corruption of the true alchemy.

It is also possible to put Mercury into modern terms. He is the *Modulator*. Modulation is the principle of impressing information onto what would otherwise be random, meaningless action in the physical world. For example, a pattern imposed upon radio waves converts the waves from being mere noise, through use of a carefully designed instrument, the radio receiver, into music or speech. Music and speech are examples of superimposing order onto intrinsically meaningless sound waves in order to give them significance in human consciousness.

Theodor Landscheidt, a philosopher and astrologer of West Germany, believes that the universe is a gigantic living system that sends data throughout itself in order to regulate itself by means of modulated gravity waves—waves generated by the inherent property of matter in that it attracts all other matter through distorting space in its vicinity. They were predicted by Einstein's theory of General Relativity, but have only recently been detected coming from the center of the galaxy by the Russians. (See Theodor Landscheidt, *Cosmic Cybernetics*, Ebertin Verlag.) If Landscheidt and the Russians are correct, this may be the first detection of the Mercurial principle operating in the physical universe at the supra-planetary level. All of the astrological symbols, I believe, must be like this; i.e., though they are manifested to us by the planetary motions within the solar system, they would also be manifested at higher and lower levels throughout the universe. This is the principle of "as above, so below" carried to its logical conclusion. We do not know what the modulator at the galactic level would be, but it must exist, and Mercury is the modulator at the planetary level of existence.

So we build our telephones, telegraphs, radios and televisions to do the same thing at the human and cultural level that Mercury does on the planetary level. As all levels of the universal symbolism run along parallel lines, the motions of the planet Mercury represent the behavior of all of these human inventions, which it rules. Of course, since the nerves carry modulated electrochemical waves around the body, they too are ruled by Mercury. They carry data to and from the brain and to the organs to regulate the response of the organism to the changes within the outer world. An interesting point here: the nerves also transmit modulated waves, which carry data that has had its origin deep within the psychic centers of the mind. This, in turn, is a creation of the psychic rather than the physical world. The nerves, therefore, also represent the only bridge between the psychic and physical halves of the universe that we can now comprehend. They are doubly Mercurial in that they are of both worlds.

In physics we find the concept of "transducers." These are devices that change modulated waves from one medium into another. A microphone, for example, changes modulated sound waves into electrical waves, which are modulated in a precisely equivalent way. A loudspeaker is a device that does the reverse, and it, too, is a transducer. Similarly, the whole speaking apparatus of the human body—the tongue, mouth, teeth, larynx, etc.—is a transducer that does the reverse. By the same token, the Mercurial principle is the transducer between the manifest and unmanifest aspects of the One.

It is a curious fact of astrology that the planets which are not visible to the naked eye—Uranus, Neptune and Pluto—are associated with factors that are unconscious or superconscious or, at any rate, alien to the normal views of consciousness. Most astrologers are not aware that the planet

Mercury is also seldom visible to the naked eye because it is usually too close to the Sun, except at maximum elongation. Even then it can be seen only under good weather conditions. I have seen Mercury only once!

So Mercury flits in and out of our world of consciousness, acting as a bridge between it and the world of primal energies as symbolized by the Sun. In so doing, Mercury connects itself to the functions of the outer planets.

The ancient alchemists appear to have been trying to return to the One via Mercury, the very gate through which the One becomes diversity. Now, in modern astrology, we have three new planets (not counting the planetoids and various "undiscovered planets"). The first is Uranus, considered by many to be the higher octave of Mercury. It shares an attribute with Mercury that may be quite significant. Like Mercury, it can also be seen with the naked eye, but only under the most favorable conditions. It can be seen very faintly in a very clear black sky when it is in opposition to the Sun. Therefore, like Mercury, it goes in and out of the world of normal consciousness. Whereas Mercury represents the route by which being comes into manifestation, perhaps Uranus and the other two outer planets represent the route by which being passes out of manifestation, the path back to the One. Uranus might represent Mercury in reverse, a transducer that leads back to the unmanifest One. If this is so, a modern alchemy will reverse the direction of its attention and study how, through Uranus, consciousness can flow out through the planets, through Uranus, Neptune, and Pluto back to the One.

All of these considerations have little to do with our practical handling of Mercury, but this is not the intent of this article. Maybe we can get a bit closer to the esoteric metaphysics which must lie at the base of the living art of astrology. Anything less and we will simply generate a new "science" of misunderstanding to take its place beside the other modern "sciences." While useful in a practical way, these sciences have served to alienate people from themselves and the experience of their own souls, and have given rise to the modern view of the universe as an accident with humans the unlucky strangers lost in the middle of it.

4

Handling the Malefics

This lecture is entitled "Handling the Malefics." The first time I gave it, I said: "This lecture should be subtitled: 'Whistling in the dark'." That is the way most people feel about it.

To be perfectly honest, I have to say at the outset that taking a pollyanna approach to the energies of these bodies is not a good idea. By pollyanna approach I mean the astrologer who looks at a client's horoscope and sees that he or she is experiencing a Saturn transit to a set of aspects in the natal chart that are rather difficult and says smilingly: "You are about to have a wonderful learning experience." I say this because I personally happen to know astrologers who have gone so far away from saying anything bad, that they don't even say anything that is real. The basic problem is malefics can be defined as those planets, statistically speaking, that most people would tend to bungle most frequently. It isn't a matter of their being inherently impossible. Because of our training, our social background, our culture, we tend not to handle these planets very well.

The planets I am talking about are Mars, Saturn, Uranus, Neptune and Pluto. First of all, none of these planets is inherently malefic when it is doing the function it is intended to do, without resistance on the part of the person in whom these functions are being done. Resistance to an energy is a large part of the problem. Resistance arises from a number of sources. Resistance basically means not allowing the energy to express itself. The first source of resistance is a conflict between what the energy signifies and what you have been taught is OK. Given this model of resistance, some can take a fairly easy aspect and mess it up. I want to give you a case in point.

If you read Alan Leo delineating a Moon square Venus, which in my book is not a particularly difficult aspect, you will find that he describes individuals as lewd, licentious, unprincipled, lustful and so forth. What it basically boils down to is this: In the Victorian Era, for a person to have a strong need for demonstrable love and affection was not socially acceptable. This transformed a perfectly low-keyed energy into something that probably was at that time genuinely difficult. To some extent I believe that a similar model can be applied to dealing with the planets that we still regard as troublesome. I think that most people don't find Mars to be all that difficult, but there are some who do. They can't handle anger. They are not willing to express negative energies, hostility, resentment, etc. Saturn, for reasons I will describe, is considered the most malefic of the group, but even there, it is mostly a matter of attitude. Uranus, Neptune and Pluto—particularly Uranus, I think—are a matter of social principles being wrong, and that is what makes the planetary energies seem hostile. Another way to define a malefic planet is: "One that often appears hostile."

Let me give you an example of resistance to Uranus. I have had a number of clients, mostly female, who have received the kind of programming about sexual role expectation that men have not. A woman comes to an astrologer with Uranus in the seventh house and says: "All I seem to be able to find are men who come into my life, sweep me off my feet and then leave me, and all I really want is a nice stable guy whom I can marry, and with whom I can have a nice house in the suburbs, raise a family, and so forth." That is an example of turning the energy malefic by resistance. The fact of the matter is that she has a strong need for freedom and elbow room in relationships, but she has been told that it is unacceptable. So there is a conflict between her role expectation, as a peaceful wife and mother in the suburbs, and what she really wants. What she does is subconsciously select only those men who will love her and leave her. She gets to have the freedom while not being wrong. Men do similar things. So the Uranus energy, which intrinsically is not that much of a problem, is rendered malefic by the fact that our personal need is in conflict with our social expectations. That is one of the most common means by which malefics are made malefic.

A second problem is that malefics relate to energies that most of us are not sufficiently competent to handle. This is more true of Uranus, Neptune and Pluto than it is of Mars and Saturn. The planets Uranus, Neptune and Pluto all have to do with issues that are outside of ordinary consciousness and experience. Let me qualify that. I am not saying that most people do not experience Uranus, Neptune and Pluto energies! Most people experience them very intensely, but they do not experience them particularly gracefully. These three planets are rendered malefic by the fact that they represent issues in consciousness that most people are not yet ready to handle. It all boils down to what Jim Eshelman said: "If we truly understood our horoscope and what it signified, we would choose to do exactly what that horoscope represents, not only natally but at any given time." The problem is that we are not really in touch with those energies. We resist them and by doing so we make them difficult.

Let me go now to a planet-by-planet breakdown of handling the malefics. Mars is among the traditional malefics. Traditionally, there are only two, Mars and Saturn. This was to balance off the traditional benefics, Venus and Jupiter. Mars was considered malefic because it related to war, violence and conflict. You have to understand that no matter how negative you may feel about the downtown area in certain cities, the probability of being physically assaulted in the Middle Ages was a great deal larger than it is now. As a matter of fact, this culture is almost boring by contrast to the Middle Ages when it comes to issues like that, which I think is why we have so much violence in our entertainment. I take the opposite position from most sociologists. I believe our taste for violence in entertainment is a result of its lack in our daily life, rather than the other way around. I think we have a certain violence quota that has to be filled somehow. Mars is the energy that defines the nature of an entity by asserting the nature of the entity; that is, Mars in my case is Mars being me. It is that energy within me that makes me assert my identity; if necessary, fight for it, but primarily just assert it, which is to say, it is me making a statement that I am such and so. It is a little more complicated than that, in that very often we will choose to sharpen the identity of ourselves by putting ourselves in conflict with someone or something. A harmless example of this is tennis, where we physically observe ourselves in competition with another individual. Any athletic competition is a relatively harmless example of Mars.

Mars is not a malefic energy at all by any stretch of the imagination. It has to do with muscular energy, vital body energy. It just so happens that if it is not handled, it handles you, which is to say that it grabs you by the throat and swings you around. Why do you suppose the violence level in this country is so high? I suggest that it is because our efforts to eliminate violence are so intense. Mars is simply the energy of "trying." We make it malefic by trying not to. I have this problem, and I am sure that many of you do also. I find it very difficult to express anger. People who are particularly repressed about Mars will eventually hold the anger in until the safety valve on the boiler, which is tied down too long, eventually causes the boiler to blow up. Some will say: "Oh my God, how difficult an energy Mars is!" Well, Venus is almost as bad if you repress it the same way.

Mars needs to have its due, and whether we choose to be physically active or psychologically aggressive, it doesn't matter, but the sense of having striven against an obstacle and survived is absolutely essential for personality development. It is our refusal to recognize this that makes Mars malefic. It is my opinion that only when your Mars has functioned at this level can you love. You can't love if you don't know who and what you are and you can't find that out unless you have striven against resistance and measured yourself against it. Winning is not the important thing, striving is! That is what Mars is all about.

When we move to Saturn we are up against a much stickier wicket. I realize that in taking this position, I am flying in the face of a very large school of pollyanna astrology which talks about Saturn as being the great, wise, wonderful, supportive teacher. I don't think that Saturn is malefic in the traditonal sense of the word. The traditional sense is "unlucky." I will acknowledge that typically it does not "feel very good" when Saturn is transiting your chart. I don't enjoy it any more than anyone else does, but I have to acknowledge that growth and knowledge come about through Saturn. Some people enjoy being taught hard lessons, other people don't, but that is not the intrinsic problem with Saturn. The intrinsic problem is that it makes you think that it is real. You lose perspective and any account of where you are.

Saturn's malefic qualities are basically the result of getting sucked into the game that the physical universe is absolute reality. If you understand Saturn as being the rules of the game that is currently being played and you take it with this sense of perspective, then you carry on the game as well as you can, because by so doing you have tacitly acknowledged that you have joined the team. If so, there is no serious problem. Except, of course, occasionally you run into the wall that says: "The rules stop here, turn around," and you say: "OK, the rules stop here. I will turn around." Or you say: "Gee, that was painful running into the wall." When you start coming to the position that the wall is out to get you, or this one, which has become extremely fashionable in some astrological circles: "I obviously sinned in a previous lifetime. That is why the wall hurt," you are in trouble. I am not a fan of certain primitive kinds of karmic astrology in which the universe is basically a cosmic bookkeeper that keeps a record of what you have done right and wrong. I do believe that actions have consequences but I believe they are much more direct than that. If you get sucked into that sort of thing, you may in fact be losing sight of what is causing the problem, which is something very concrete and definite.

Another problem with Saturn relates to this. Saturn ultimately has to do with the consensus idea of reality. The criterion for that concept of reality is that everybody says what is real is that which tends to alienate you from your own experience. How many of you believe in the existence of the unconscious mind? Would you care to prove that there is such a thing as an unconscious mind? Why do you believe in it?

If you define unconscious mind as the place where memory goes when you don't remember it, that is an experiential explanation. I don't quarrel with that. But let us talk about your secretly hating your father. You say: "Well there may be something to that. I haven't seen him in a number of years and I am not too crazy about writing to him," and the psychologist says sagely: "See, I told you." Or scenario number two: "That is not true. I see my father regularly, we are good friends. We talk a lot. We get together. We have a lot of things in common," and the psychologist says: "See, you are overcompensating for guilt."

I am not taking a position on the reality of the subconscious mind. My point is that there are a lot of ideas that we believe simply because we have been told they are true. A lot of things get into consensus reality that have nothing to do with anybody's experience. They just happen to be authoritative statements of people whom we are convinced are authoritative. This is one effect when Saturn alienates us from our experience. We create a consensus idea of reality that has very little to do with our experience. This is what I mean about Saturn's most malefic quality, which is that it makes you think that its effects are real.

Now let's get down to the practical issue. How do we deal with a heavy Saturnine energy? First of all, it is incumbent on you to get centered. When I say centered, I mean to get a sense of internal balance and equilibrium so that you can get in touch with what is real for you. What do you really want and need? Realistically, given the rules of the game, how can you manipulate things so that your needs are met, instead of saying, "I can't do it because of this or that"; or "What will they say if I do this? Do I really want to stand out in a crowd by doing something unusual?" All of these are Saturnine considerations.

A Mars-Saturn contact may signify nothing more than a need to start proceeding very slowly in a detailed manner with a great deal of attention because clearly that kind of combination does not permit tremendous thrusts of unlimited energy. There has got to be a certain amount of planning and caution involved.

A Saturn-Venus experience may get you in touch with the fact that you have considerations by which you have made it impossible to be in love with someone. You may, for example, have a tendency to fall in love with people who live on the other side of the continent, and aren't planning to move to be near you. Or you may have a tendency to fall in love with people who are thirty years older, are married and have no plans to leave a spouse. Or you may have decided that being in love has so many burdens and responsibilities that it is easier to be alone, even if it isn't pleasant. So we create these elaborate psychological structures that determine our activity, but, again, if you really look at it from the proper perspective, these structures have no reality whatsoever.

My favorite aphorism is that Saturn is the illusion that there is a reality, and Neptune is the truth that there isn't. I think the most important word is "a"...there is *a* reality. As I have said, I am a believer in the multiple universe theory. If you can get clear that Saturn is the rules of the game that you have voluntarily chosen to participate in, and that you can, if you understand them thoroughly, manipulate these rules to your own ends and satisfaction, Saturn periods are not that difficult. Usually, we lose perspective. We get totally sucked in and find Saturn to be a terrifyingly negative experience. However, being in touch with the rules of the game is the positive aspect of Saturn. Not realizing that it is a game is the negative aspect.

I hear you saying: "What about the person who gets caught in a mass tragedy of some sort and whose life is snuffed out or made miserable?" I think you will find that these people are not enjoying Saturn transits. They are enjoying transits of the three outer planets. If Saturn is in there, it is usually not by itself.

The problem with Uranus has already been alluded to in the story of the woman with the powerful Uranus who wanted a stable relationship. You have to understand that Uranus operates outside of the normal consensus reality, that is, the reality of Saturn. Its function is simple and important. As Saturn increasingly structures one's reality system, it also tends to cut the person off from life energies. This is seen in ordinary life in the hardening of the arteries and general loss of flexibility that occurs in old age. In breaking through the conventional rules, Uranus enables vital energies to come back through into life. Most people find that they feel renewed when they have successfully withstood events that are disruptive and strange to them.

Using our game metaphor again, Saturn tends to cause the game to be played again and again in exactly same way. As it does so, the game loses interest for the players. There is no challenge in it anymore. Uranus comes through in those moments when someone discovers a new way of playing the game that renews the sense of excitement and interest that has been lost. However, there are usually two completely different sets of reactions to such moments. Some people will immediately feel the renewed energy. Others will feel that the rules themselves have been violated and the game is in danger. Those who feel this will dig in their heels and refuse to accept the new release of energy that has come forth. For them, Uranus is immediately a malefic. If these conservatives win out and consistently do so, tensions will begin to arise as the forces of new life begin to build up pressure. If the forces of Saturn win out frequently enough, the forces of Uranus will eventually break through with terrible, destructive force. At this point Uranus will be perceived as a malefic by almost everyone involved.

The central problem with Uranus is that it takes courage to resist the forces of reaction, both in oneself and in others, and to allow the energies to manifest. Commonly it is within oneself that the problem is most serious. Most of us are afraid of change and will not act to release Uranian forces until the pressure cooker has begun to build up. In the body, resisted Uranian energy may manifest itself as a sudden outbreak of violent emotions, a sudden breakdown in the body (heart attacks for example) or as accidents. Often the breakthrough of energy is so severe that it causes distortion. By merely looking at the manifestation we cannot see what caused the buildup in the first place. We have to look at the symbolism of the breakdown. Only then can we see the original roots of the problem. For example, a heart attack is literally a broken heart. Perhaps it is also metaphorically a broken heart. The heart is symbolized in astrology by the Sun. The Sun is self-expression. Perhaps the individual has gone on so long working so hard to fulfill the expectations of others, that he or she has had no time to allow his or her own wants to be met. Therefore, the heart (Sun) breaks.

All we have to do to make Uranus work is to give it room. We have to remain in touch with ourselves and our innermost needs, expressing them when they need to be expressed. The balance that we have within us between Saturn and Uranus will help us distinguish between self-indulgence and necessary self-expression.

Now we move to Neptune. I have a good friend who is a professional astrologer and a psychic. While driving home from a long series of seminars she had a vision of an earthquake occurring to the south of Cape Cod, creating a giant tidal wave and overwhelming Martha's Vineyard and the south shore of Cape Cod. She saw the date on which this was going to occur, which I am happy to report was a couple of months ago and nothing happened. Now, was she wrong? If you mean was there going to be an earthquake and tidal wave, the answer is "No there wasn't, she was wrong." But that is the typical kind of question we ask of Neptune, whereas we ought to be asking: "What does the vision mean?" At that time she was having difficult problems with her parents, who live on Cape Cod. I am not saying that the earthquake was going to drown them. That is not the point. In the course of seeing this vision she got very excited and agitated. All day long she had been doing psychic readings, to the point where her normal ego consciousness had become completely overwhelmed by the forces she had been dealing with. What she had been experiencing, I believe, was a visual perception of the dangers of her own ego being drowned by the energies she aroused.

I may be totally wrong about that interpretation. All I am trying to say here is that it is much more valuable to try to figure out what Neptune means than to try to figure out what is "real"—more valuable to flow with it, to allow it to be the intrusion of a divine energy into normal reality—even if it is a not-so-pleasant divine energy. But the ultimate strategy of dealing with Neptune involves a process of conscious surrender and allowing the energy to use you, almost as a medium, for whatever end it may require. For the most part I think we would deal with Neptune much more creatively if we surrendered to it and kept some sense of perspective about who we are and what we are doing. We should also remember that this Neptunian thing is the game whose rules we tacitly acknowledge we are going to follow. So it is perfectly legitimate to say: "I am playing soccer but I acknowledge that there is validity in basketball." Neptune is the intrusion of the rules of basketball into a soccer game. It may also be a perception that the fullback on the other side is playing hockey somewhere else. Which brings us to Pluto.

Pluto is another energy that requires detachment and an incredible amount of flexibility. The way we treat schizophrenia is more applicable to Pluto than to Uranus because it is in fact Pluto that most often signifies that kind of a breakdown. When we get in touch with Pluto symbolism it becomes clear that a lot of schizophrenia is a death and rebirth experience. I don't care if there are chemical imbalances. Who said that the chemical imbalances caused the schizophrenia? It may perfectly well be the other way around. Breakdowns that occur during Pluto transits, whatever they are, are breakdowns that are best not resisted. It is a good idea to jettison whatever there is to jettison at that time. Get rid of it, throw it out, and as with Uranus go through it as rapidly as possible, consistent with getting the job done. You have to understand that Pluto is a very powerful energy of transformation that occurs as a result of the internal structure of the entity that is breaking down. Pluto is not the result of an external force intervening. It is inherent in the very process that gave birth to it. An example of this is earthquakes. When the earthquake occurs it is Uranian; but the force behind it is Plutonian.

Death is the so far inevitable result of normal biological processes. No external interference is required. Things tend to break down. It is part of the law of Nature, which suggests that the best thing to do about that is to die. I don't mean to force the issue, but get it over with and go on to whatever happens next. I believe that in any Plutonian experience, not just death, the best thing is to have it and finish it.

There is another aspect to Pluto, which is terribly important, and that is, if you yourself are Plutonian, what do you do with that energy? Well, I'll tell you what you don't do with it. You don't bend it to your own purposes. I don't know if we have any practitioners of ritual magic in the room. I would like to make my position clear on that subject. I don't think it is supernatural if supernatural means going beyond nature. If it can happen, it is natural. Magic is essentially a very disciplined and careful martialing of psychic energies so that they can be directed to any objective. Here comes the rub. This is a Plutonian art because what first has to be mastered completely is *will, power, energy,* and then a transformation occurs. Magic in its highest form is clearly a form of yoga. Yoga in general is a way of achieving union with the divine. It is not twisting your muscles into a strange shape. Its pitfall is the seduction of the ego. There is a point in the development of magical skills where you get to the point where you say: "Gee look at all these weird things I can do...far out!" The problem there is, when you get to that point you have to be able to use them not for your own amusement.

Pluto could be called a yang Neptune. You quietly slide away from Neptune and things seem to improve a little bit at least. With Pluto you have to say consciously: "I give this power that I have to the service of the universe, and to the growth of my own soul." For example, a fairly common Plutonian profession is therapy. Any kind of therapy is Plutonian: physical therapy, psychotherapy, rolfing and so forth. If you don't believe it, spend some time doing the horoscopes of psychiatrists and watch the eighth house, Scorpio and Pluto swing out. When I did a number of these charts I found all these Jupiter and Pluto conjunctions wandering around the place. Of course, that is a particularly healing energy.

Anyone who is in the business of assisting people is in a Plutonian profession. That is a positive use of Pluto. But suppose instead of assisting people in their transformation, you made them transform for your own ends in some way, when it wasn't appropriate for it to happen. Magic teaches that you will get it back in the face, doubled! This is not purely restricted to something as debatable as the existence of magic.

Let us look at political ambition. Richard Nixon has Pluto in the tenth house opposition the triple conjunction of Mars, Mercury and Jupiter. I believe that gives him sound Plutonian credentials. One can argue, although I am not inclined to, whether or not he deserved to be thrown out of office. He was thrown out because of the peculiarly relentless, Plutonian style of pursuing his ends. All the way from Helen Gahagan Douglas forward, he systematically set about creating a set of enemies who eventually grew more powerful than he was, and he kept giving them the tools until finally they out-Plutoed him. If you take a Plutonian energy in your life and subject it to narrow, personal, egotistical ends, the energy will get you. Usually in the form of people who are out for your hide.

There are some things here that I can't account for, such as the nonsensical, weird tragedies that afflict people for no obvious reason. I can only say that the reasons are not obvious. I can only point out that when human beings write plays, the best ones are tragedies. It is obviously something we have in our nature to make us relish a good cry. So we are just as likely to engineer something brutal and horrible as we are something sweet, lovely and light.

Given a society that is reasonably stable, it is my belief that in ordinary life the tragedy that comes from malefics results from our not dealing with the malefic in a way that is appropriate to the nature of the planet. As such, "malefic" energies are manageable. I also firmly believe that most of us would probably fail to manage them, but we can at least try.

5

Geocentric Latitude:
Some Second Thoughts

One point on which technique-minded astrologers have prided themselves is the use of geocentric rather than geographic latitude when calculating the Ascendant and house cusps of a horoscope. This article is a thorough inquiry into the subject of the proper latitude to use, and will come up with an answer that may surprise many.

Defining the Ascendant

In order to deal with this question we must first agree on what the Ascendant is. Most astrologers have a general idea: The Ascendant/Descendant axis is a line formed by the intersection of the plane of the ecliptic with the plane of the horizon. When these two planes are projected onto the celestial sphere, they become circles, and the two places where these circles intersect become the Ascendant and Descendant points. For the purposes of this discussion, let us put down a precise, rigorous and geometric definition: *The Ascendant is the point formed in the east by the intersection of the circle of the ecliptic with the circle of the rational or geocentric horizon.*

The only thing that might not appear to be completely understandable here is the term "rational or geocentric horizon" (the two words are used interchangeably). This is defined in Simon Newcomb's *Compendium of Spherical Astronomy* (1906; reprint ed., New York: Dover Publications, 1960, p.92) as follows:

> The plane of the horizon, or horizontal plane, is defined as that which is perpendicular to the direction of gravity at any place, or to the direction of the plumbline.

Further on, Newcomb states:

> A distinction is sometimes made between the horizontal plane passing through the position of the observer, and the parallel plane passing through the center of the earth. The first is called the *apparent*; the second, the *rational* or *geocentric* horizon. The distinction is unnecessary on the horizon of the infinite sphere, because the two planes cut the sphere in coincident circles.

(The apparent or local horizon is assumed to be at sea level.) Thus the rational horizon referred to in the definition of the Ascendant can be thought of as a plane that passes through the center of the earth; this is why it is also called the "geocentric" horizon. The word "geocentric" here has given rise to some confusion, as we shall see.

Types of Latitude

If the earth were a perfect sphere, there would be no problem about latitude: geographic and geocentric would be the same. But in fact the earth is slightly flattened at the poles. Depending on whether or not this flattening is taken into account, there are two principal ways of measuring latitude:

1. Geographic and astronomical latitude assume that the earth is perfectly spherical:
    A. *Astronomical latitude* is the angle between a plumbline held at any spot on the earth and a plumbline held at the equator. It is derived directly from observation.
    B. *Geographic latitude* is the same as astronomical latitude, except that it is very slightly corrected for local gravitational fluctuations. This is the latitude that is given in atlases.

    Astronomical and geographic latitude rarely vary more than 30″ from each other, and for the purposes of this discussion they are identical.

2. *Geocentric latitude* takes the flattening at the earth's poles into account, and can vary from geographic latitude by as much as 12′. It is defined as the angle between a line drawn from the observer to the center of the earth and a line drawn from the equator to the center of the earth. This is not determined directly from observation but is derived from the geographic latitude by means of a trigonometric equation that compensates for the lack of sphericity of the earth.

Geographic vs. Geocentric

The two principal ways of defining latitude give rise to two ways of defining the zenith:

1. The *astronomical/geographic zenith*, created by extending the plumbline infinitely upward through the celestial sphere, and

2. The *geocentric zenith*, created by extending an imaginary line from the observer to the center of the earth infinitely upward through the celestial sphere.

Figure 1 illustrates this principle. For the purposes of this discussion the flatness of the earth at the poles is greatly exaggerated, but the principle is geometrically correct.

Now, let there be an observer at point *P* on the surface of the earth. If the observer holds a plumbline it will point in the direction *PM*, which is exactly perpendicular to the surface of the spheroid at *P*. Note that *M* is not the center of the earth, which is at *O*. Angle *PMX*, which is indicated by Ø, corresponds to the astronomical/geographical latitude. Angle *POX*, indicated by Ø', corresponds to the geocentric latitude. *PM* extended upward shows the astronomical/geographic zenith, *Z*, while *PO* extended upward shows the geocentric zenith, *Z'*.

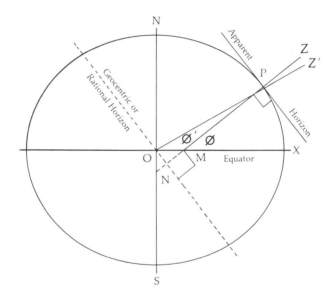

Figure 1. Line *ZN*, which represents the direction that the plumbline will take, is at right angles to both the apparent horizon and the geocentric or rational horizon. But only at the equator and the poles will it point to the center of the earth.

Here is the critical point. As we can see, a line drawn tangent to the spheroid at point *P* is in fact the apparent horizon, and by definition it is perpendicular to *ZPM*. Also by the definition of Newcomb (and everyone else) it is parallel to the geocentric or rational horizon, which passes through the center of the earth. But because the geocentric horizon is parallel to the apparent horizon, it is not perpendicular to *PO*. Rather, it is perpendicular to *PM* extended downward to point *N*. Thus, although the geocentric horizon is geocentric, it is not established by the geocentric latitude. The geocentric horizon is established by the astronomical/geographic latitude—which is what is gotten off a map with no further alteration.

Thus, if the Ascendant is indeed determined by the intersection of the plane of the geocentric horizon with the plane of the ecliptic in the east, then the astronomical/geographic latitude is the correct one to use. Geocentric latitude would only be the correct one to use if we changed the definition of the Ascendant to the intersection of the ecliptic with a horizon that is perpendicular to line *PO*. But the apparent horizon would then be tangent to the earth's surface at some other point than *P*.

It seems that the use of geocentric latitude is astrologically valid for only one purpose, calculating parallax, most notably of the Moon. But this is a correction that almost everyone disregards at present (whether rightly or wrongly no one knows at this point).

Those who have heard me lecture or who have read my book *Planets in Composite* (Gloucester, Mass.: Para Research, 1975, p. 15) will realize that this is a change of position on my part. I, too, have advocated using geocentric latitude until very recently. This was because along with many other astrologers, I had been under a misapprehension about the definitions of geocentric horizon and geographic or astronomical latitude.

The error was first pointed out to me by John Kahila and A.H. Blackwell, technically very skillful astrologers who work in the sidereal zodiac. As a result of their statements, I went into my spherical astronomy texts and found the material that I have recounted here. Astronomers, not being very concerned about the calculation of the Ascendant, have not made the issue crystal clear, but rigorous argument from the correct astronomical definitions makes it quite plain that what I have indicated here is the case. This is not a new discovery, but it is a point that has too often been overlooked.

Postscript—July, 1982

The original article printed above gives the technical, astronomical reasons for not using geocentric latitude. What follows is a discussion of the consequences for practical astrology.

In the main body of the article, I pointed out that the geocentric horizon is determined by a plane passing through the center of the Earth perpendicular to the plumbline at a particular spot. The latitude that results from the measure is astronomical latitude. I then pointed out that for all practical purposes this is the same as geographical latitude, the value given in most atlases and used by most astrologers. This is because the average curvature of the Earth on which geographic latitude is based is almost within a minute of arc of being the same as plumbline latitude (astronomical). However, to be theoretically correct you should, in fact, refer to astronomical latitude not geographic. Normally this is of no consequence except that it might help to solve a problem that has vexed technically-minded astrologers for some time. What do you do for children born in deep valleys, or on mountains, or worse yet in airplanes or even space satellites? In all of these cases the visible horizon does not come even close to the rational horizon. For those born on mountains or in airplanes there is tremendous dip so that the visible horizon does not divide the celestial sphere into two equal hemispheres. Those born in valleys have the opposite problem.

Most astrologers have simply ignored the problem and gone on computing Ascendants as if the normal kind of horizon were in effect. This has bothered the technically minded. They seem to feel that the visible intersection of the earth with the sky in the east should be the basis of the Ascendant, not some abstract mathematical entity, i.e. the rational horizon. However, once again I think the technical astrologers have been incorrect and the average astrologer correct, if unaware of the reasons for being correct. To determine this we have to go back to the definition of the astronomical horizon as the plane that is perpendicular to the plumbline.

What does this mean? It means that the astronomical horizon consists of a plane cutting the celestial sphere, a plane which is perpendicular to the gravitational vector at any spot on earth. If you imagine a line of force connecting you to the Earth, which is the gravitational pull of the Earth, then you can see what we have in mind. Simply imagine a plane perpendicular to that line and you have the horizon. Now most of us do not believe that gravity is the operational force behind astrology. Many of us do not even believe that there are any operational forces behind astrology in the usual physical sense of the word. However, is it not reasonable to suppose that whatever is behind astrology would operate in a manner similar to gravity?

The positions of the planets in the chart are essentially the directions of lines drawn from the center of the earth to the planets. The planets are so far away that there is no distinction between lines drawn to their geometrical centers and those drawn to their mass centers. However, as the article has shown, there is such a distinction with the Earth. The direction from the individual to the geometrical center determines geocentric latitude, and the direction to the mass center determines astronomical latitude.

If we accept the ideas given above, then the horizon consists of those points that are in mundane square to the gravitational vector of the Earth at any point. The Ascendant then is the point of the ecliptic in the east that is in mundane square to the Earth's gravitational vector. (Of course the Ascendant is not always in the east if you accept the principles set forth in the article, "The Ascendant, Midheaven and Vertex in Extreme Latitudes.")

This gives an astrological definition to the horizon as well as an astronomical one. This means that we find a horizon, and therefore an

Ascendant, as long as we can trace a gravitational vector between ourselves and the Earth. This can be done in an airplane, or even a space satellite, so long as we are not too far from the Earth. Persons in interplanetary space probably would have to use a gravitational vector to the Sun rather than the Earth. They would also have to use heliocentric positions rather than geocentric positions. I think the problem has been that under normal conditions the definition of the horizon in terms of the visible division that it gives (the apparent horizon) and the definition in terms of perpendicularity to gravity (the astronomical horizon) give almost exactly the same results. However, under extreme conditions the two definitions give divergent results. I believe the gravitational definition is the correct one to use.

6

On Creating a Science of Astrology

The attack on astrology last fall by *The Humanist* (see Bart J. Bok, "A Critical Look at Astrology," and Lawrence E. Jerome, "Astrology: Magic or Science?", *The Humanist*, September-October 1975) contains much that is clearly false and much that is simply allegation, as many readers will be quick to see. But rather than dissect the articles of Dr. Bok and Mr. Jerome point by point, I think it more important, and more interesting, to discuss some basic issues that these articles raise.

Astrology Not Yet a Science

First of all, Dr. Bok is incorrect in calling astrology a pseudoscience. Up until now, astrology has not been a science at all—not even an erroneous one. It has been a craft or technology, which is quite different.

A science in the strict sense of the word is an inquiry into pure truth, using a set of deductive and inductive procedures loosely known as the scientific method. While the precise method of inquiry varies from science to science, there are certain elements in common. All use particular facts or observations to suggest general principles or theories, which are then referred back to a different set of facts for confirmation. There is a well-ordered dialogue between nature and the scientist.

The important thing is that pure knowledge is the object of science—there is no immediate interest in applying it to the manipulation of the universe—and this knowledge is gathered in a systematic way. Crafts and technologies, on the other hand, apply knowledge to practical problems, and their knowledge is not necessarily gathered systematically.

We must remember that science and technology were not always related as closely as they are now. In modern times the distinction between these two activities has been obscured by the tremendous influence that the sciences have come to exert on the crafts and technologies, but prior to 150 years ago the crafts existed quite independently of science. Science did not supply them with knowledge as it now does; if anything, it was the other way around. One did not study metallurgy in order to become a blacksmith, but a blacksmith's experience with iron might have given metallurgists some clues.

Craftsmen got their knowledge from a simple "cut and try" approach, which made no theoretical statements. These people were not interested, except secondarily, in why something worked—they only wanted to know that it did. Nevertheless, such technologies could be quite effective; in fact, they often made discoveries that scientists could not make, because the craftsmen were not blinded by theoretical formulations that precluded making the observation in the first place. But the technological approach was also limited by its concentration on practice rather than truth, so that along with the valuable material, it took in much that was superfluous or erroneous.

Now astrology, too, is in at least one sense an empirically derived craft, devised for practical ends. What time should one get married, for example, or start a business? Knowledge has been gathered piecemeal to answer such questions, and related to theory only in a non-rigorous way. It works reasonably well, but it has not been strictly tested in a search for the truth, and it has little or no theory in the scientific sense of basic principles that have been discovered to account for all the empirical evidence at hand. As with the early crafts, the practice of astrology may yield some valuable knowledge to a new science of astrology, but it probably also contains much that will one day prove invalid.

Astrology is in a similar position to modern psychotherapy—especially the schools of Freud, Adler, Jung, et al.—which has been derived almost entirely from day-to-day experience with patients, and which depends on theoretical structures that are hard to verify in a rigorous manner. Prediction on the basis of these theories of personality has been at least as unreliable as astrological prediction, yet the treatment is accepted as having some value. The reason that astrology is not accepted and modern psychotherapy is, I submit, is that the ideas of astrologers are in conflict with today's prevailing metaphysical assumptions, whereas those of the psychologists (except possibly Jung) are not.

The Metaphysical Bases of Astrology

This brings us to the second issue. There must be a reason why scientists such as Dr. Bok take the time and energy to denounce astrology. Why is it so important to them; why is their tone so high-pitched; and what prevents these obviously intelligent people from adequately researching the subject they wish to condemn? The answer, I think, is that astrology threatens the conceptual structure through which they are accustomed to view the world. Astrology can't be right; for if it were, then the metaphysical basis on which most scientists operate today would be wrong. Conversely, if the basis on which most scientists found their structure is right, then astrology must be absurd. It is this logic that allows 186 scientists to state with such insouciance that astrology is nonsense, when most of them have not even investigated the subject.

Let us remember that, like most people, the majority of scientists are not aware of the extent to which their observations are organized by their metaphysical assumptions. When they are conscious of these assumptions, they consider them to be "common sense" or necessary for any empirical investigation. What they do not realize is that "common sense" differs from century to century and culture to culture. Thomas Kuhn in *The Structure of Scientific Revolutions* (Chicago: University of Chicago Press, 1970) describes how philosophical paradigms change from age to age for reasons which historians have never adequately explained. If one examines metaphysical revolutions, one sees that the greatest occurred at just about the time astrology went out of favor; and that, I maintain, is *why* it went out of favor.

What, precisely, is the difference between the basic assumptions of most people today, including scientists, and those of the astrologers?

For one thing, from the late Renaissance until this century a mechanical, cause-and-effect view of the universe has prevailed. Even now, after Einstein, it stubbornly persists. In this view there is a definite order of events in the universe, such that there can be a set of events, *A*, which uniquely and peculiarly determines another set of events, *B*. *A* is cause and *B*, effect. But in fact it is impossible to demonstrate that there is ever a perfect determinism between any set of causes and effects. And if you accept general relativity, there is not even a unique order of events. The order of events depends upon the observer's location in the time-space continuum. In other words, the perception of cause and effect is, in the final analysis, subjective. All you can say about events that are "causes" and events that are "effects" is that there is a highly reliable correlation between them. The cause-and-effect model suffices for most of the science being done today, and scientists are apt to extend it from their daily work to their entire world-view and assume that everyone else must do likewise. They should remember that in sciences such as particle physics this concept does not suffice.

And yet astrology is still attacked on the basis of this superseded view. Scientists ridicule astrologers for believing that the planets, so remote from us, could actually have measurable physical effects on us and *cause* things to happen here on earth. In fact, there is some evidence for correlation between planetary movement and physical events on the Sun and the Earth, and a cause-and-effect energy connection may eventually be found to explain these correlations—but it is not *necessary* that astrology work according to the cause-and-effect model. There are other ways of looking at it, as some of the newer developments in physics suggest. Carl Jung and the physicist Wolfgang Pauli have set forth an alternative way in the concept of synchronicity (see "Synchronicity: An Acausal Connecting Principle," in *The Structure and Dynamics of the Psyche* [Princeton, 1969]).

Another difference between the world-views of scientists and astrologers is that most scientists and other people today assume that reality lies in the object—i.e., that which exists independently of any observer and which can be viewed in more or less the same way by any observer. The objectivist considers experiences that are created or conditioned by the nature of the individual to be unreal, imaginary, or at best "subjective"—i.e., of an inferior order of reality.

Such a view has given rise to a theory of creation in which living organisms are formed solely through the chance interaction of matter and energy. Eventually consciousness comes into being through the same laws of physics, chemistry, and probability that gave rise to organisms. Thus in the modern creation story the object precedes consciousness, and matter and energy precede all.

But so far this theory of creation has not been rigorously demonstrated. And, by the very nature of the question, the metaphysical assumption on which it is based can never be proved. Thus, other metaphysical assumptions are quite possible, and equally unprovable. You could just as well assume that reality lies not in objects but in consciousness.

Astrology survives from an age in which consciousness and mind (not necessarily human mind) were thought to permeate nature, and in which no clear boundary was drawn between the observer and the observed. In such a world-view one *experiences* both oneself and not-self, but this experience is recognized to take place entirely within the individual. There *may* be a universe out there, but what we experience of it is entirely within us. The experience may be *determined* by what is out there, but such a statement is not verifiable by direct observation because it itself is about observation. Ultimately it is a metaphysical statement that cannot be proved.

Astrology assumes that the universe is composed of the same principles as those that make up the individual psyche. Therefore it is logical to assume that there will be a correlation between the behavior of one part, the heavens, and the behavior of another, the individual. No causal mechanism is required. When perceived through the structure of the human consciousness, planets follow the same archetypal principles as people, or anything else in the universe; hence looking at one realm gives clues to the behavior of the other. Indeed, scientific discovery itself often arises from the tendency of the human mind to make analogies between one part of nature and another. Similarly, so does self-discovery arise from analogies between planets and parts of the psyche or events in the life. This is the "principle of correspondences" that Jerome refers to, here placed in its proper philosophical setting. This principle is only *a priori* absurd when viewed in our contemporary metaphysical framework. Though it is mystical in the strict sense of the word, it is not irrational. Once you accept the unprovable basic assumption, unprovable like all such assumptions, it has its own internal logic. It does not permit everything to be true; just as much as the prevailing view does, it limits the possible manifestations within the universe.

The above description is not intended to convince the reader that this world-view is correct and that the orthodox, objectivist view is wrong. It is only intended to give some idea of where astrology is coming from. It is important to note that there is no empirical way directly to judge the truth of one view over the other. Whatever metaphysical view is chosen, it is still an article of faith whether you are a scientist or an astrologer.

But the present-day popularity of Eastern religion, astrology and the other branches of the occult signifies that this other view of reality is coming back. We may be in the midst of another metaphysical revolution. In itself this is neither good nor bad. But those whose careers, livelihoods, reputations, and even sanity depend upon the established way of looking at things are bound to be made uncomfortable, and hence to protest.

The Testing of Astrology

Although astrology arises from a different metaphysical basis than does present-day science, this does not preclude using scientific method to verify astrological hypotheses. I said before that up to the present astrology has been a craft, and that astrology as a science has never existed before, but nowadays such a science is beginning to be generated.

Contrary to what Mr. Jerome says, astrologers are not latching onto science just because it is respectable and they can use its findings to gain status in the eyes of the public. True, astrologers would like the comfort of more toleration from the rest of society, and the benefits that might come from this, such as funding and access to academic facilities, which would greatly speed the progress of astrological knowledge. They realize that to gain such acceptance they, not the scientists, have the obligation to prove their hypotheses using the methods of science. But they would also like to test their practices rigorously in order to make their craft work better. And some would like to do basic research—not to test established practices, but to explore, for the sake of pure knowledge, whatever correlations there may be between cosmic events and life on earth. It is from this latter type of research that astrology is most likely to derive any general theories in the scientific sense.

It is unfortunate that most astrologers are out of touch with the basic-research aspect of astrology, and of those who are in touch with it, many feel threatened by it. The serious journals of astrology contain a mixture of articles relating to the craft of astrology and a very few relating to astrology truly as a science. Possibly the reason for "scientific" astrology's unpopularity is that it seems irrelevant to the practical, everyday concerns of the average counseling astrologer: the mind is only willing to endure a limited amount of distraction from its main object of interest. Moreover, if research comes up with results that are contrary to the techniques by which astrologers have been working, the cognitive dissonance that arises is painful, disrupting, and inconvenient. It is quite possible that some of the ideas we cherish may turn out to be wrong. The only thing that we feel sure of is that the basic idea of astrology is sound—that there are cyclical correlations between the various levels of reality (microcosm and macrocosm) which can be used to increase our understanding of humanity and nature conjointly.

Whether we are verifying established techniques or exploring new concepts, the testing of astrology presents some special problems. Astrologers are only just now learning to test their own practices. Most of us have not had the proper training to do so. So far, the testing of astrology has been done by a few dedicated amateurs with no funding. We have recently realized that this whole development has been awaiting computers to sort out the tremendous number of variables involved, and only now do we finally have the use of them.

Another problem is that astrology by its very nature is hard to test. Inasmuch as it involves subjective factors, it is as hard to tackle as psychology. And even if we decide to test only easily verifiable facts such as suicides or choice of profession, the assessment of the astrological factors still depends not on separate parts, but upon many factors taken together. Most early tests, including those of Gauquelin, always took one element out of context for testing. Although this can yield interesting results, as it has in Gauquelin's correlation between professions and the positions of certain planets, research into the synthesizing techniques of astrology has awaited more sophisticated approaches such as the statistical analysis of many variables at once.

Statistics, however, on which so much of our research depends, has a notoriously rubbery nature. As a perusal of any journal, especially in the social sciences, will show, investigators constantly argue about the validity of each others' statistical models. This was obvious in the criticisms of Rhine's work on ESP. It is very difficult to get someone, on the basis of statistical arguments, to accept results that the person is unwilling to accept. Results favorable to one's work are examined cursorily, whereas ones that are not favorable are scrutinized with care. I am not accusing anyone of bad faith. I am only suggesting that all investigators are human, and that the popular image of the scientist with his ego serenely detached from his work is quite an exaggeration. And most scientists know this. At any rate this is a special problem for astrologers because of the strangeness of our ideas.

Conclusion

The writers in *The Humanist* are upset because they think that the resurgence of astrology and related beliefs portends a new Dark Ages. But the earlier view is not returning in exactly the same form to undo all that science has achieved. Astrologers do not deny that something valuable has been accomplished in the last few centuries by the objectivist world-view. But it is now becoming apparent that though this view is useful for some things, it does not explain all of life. When you get to very small magnitudes (subatomic particles) and very large ones (the universe as a whole), or even when you consider some aspects of human behavior ("psychic" phenomena), objectivist science begins to lose its power to describe and predict, and studies start resembling metaphysics more than science.

Likewise, for certain sorts of geocosmic correlations (such as those of planetary positions and short-wave radio reception) a cause-and-effect energy basis may one day be found that will satisfy the most hard-nosed objectivist. But for other astrological phenomena (such as the symbolic connection the planets seem to have with human life) we may have to revise our conception of reality.

The task of astrological research is not to alter this concept too readily, without giving stringent scrutiny to all possible explanations. If astrological research can prove beyond doubt in a strict, skeptical, Saturnian manner that the world is stranger than objectivist science can compass, it will indeed have contributed to the expansion of human understanding.

7

A New Approach to Transits

What I am putting forth in this article is a new manner of dealing with transits. It is both conceptually and operationally new and contains some startling implications for astrological methodology and theory. Unlike most such theories, it is based on experimentally verified fact and worked out according to mathematical models. In practice it is still in the testing stages, but the purpose of this article is to alert others to this approach and to ask astrologers to assist me in working out the details and in verifying certain principles that will be mentioned later on in the course of the article.

The starting point for this whole inquiry was the work of Michel Gauquelin, particularly the research showing the correlation between planetary angularity and various professions. By way of refreshing the reader's memory, Gauquelin discovered that the charts of large samples of members of several professions showed planets that have traditionally been connected with those professions to have just transited the east and west horizon and the upper and lower meridian circle to a degree that is statistically highly significant. Rather than refer to this work in detail here, I refer the reader to Gauquelin's several works in English for a description of the various tests and their results. (See Michel Gauquelin, *Cosmic Influences on Human Behavior*, New York: Stein and Day, 1973.)

What I found to be significant is that in each case a diurnal intensity cycle was detected in which each of the planets peaked four times a day, immediately after a transit of one of the four angles. This creates an irregular rhythm, because, depending on its particular declination circle, a planet transits the four angles of the mundane sphere at irregular intervals. The geometry of the mundane sphere is such that a given planet will transit the upper and lower meridian roughly twelve hours apart, but the rising and setting transits will have no fixed relationship to each other or to the meridian transits. The only thing that is definite is that the meridian transits will occur halfway in time between rising and setting. A simple example can be found with the Sun, which, of course, gives rise to daylight and night in varying proportions throughout the year.

On January 20, 1976 at 40°N latitude the Sun rose at 7:18 u.t. meridian of Greenwich and set at 17:04 u.t. meridian of Greenwich. The Sun transited the meridian at 12:11 u.t. meridian of Greenwich. This gives daylight a time of 9:45. Half of this time is 4:53, which added to the sunrise time of 7:18 u.t. gives 12:11 u.t., the time of the Sun's transit of the meridian. On July 18, 1976 the Sun rose at 4:46 u.t. and set at 19:26 u.t., both times for meridian of Greenwich and 40°N as before. Here we have a total daylight time of 14:40 and the midpoint in time of that duration is 12:06 u.t., the time of the Sun's transit over the local meridian.

What is true for the Sun is true for all bodies, i.e. that the times of the meridian transits are always close to twelve hours apart (the Moon because of its rapid zodiacal motion may vary more than this) and the times of rising and setting are variable with respect to the times of the meridian transits. However, they are always symmetrical in time with respect to the meridian, such that risings and settings are equidistant in time from the meridian transits. These peaks of intensity are graphically represented in figure 1. The exact location of the peaks is not clear except that they are somewhere just past the transits of the angles. Please note here that we are always referring to the bodily transits of the horizon circle and the meridian circles, not the zodiacal positions of the Ascendant, Midheaven, Descendant and Imum Coeli. This is in keeping with Gauquelin's procedure.

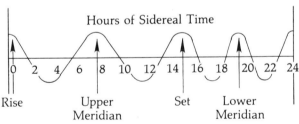

Figure 1. Patty Hearst Natal Uranus Diurnal Rhythm. Here is the diurnal wave of Patty Hearst's natal Uranus. The peaks are placed precisely at the angle transits, which is not exactly in accord with Gauquelin's data, but the effect would be similar to Gauquelin's if one moved the peaks slightly into the areas of the cadent houses. The wave is generated by taking the cosine of the fourth harmonic of the mundane position of the planet plotted against sidereal time as the horizontal coordinate. The mundane position we calculated by projecting the planet at twenty-minute intervals onto the equator using great circles extending from the north point to the south point of the horizon.

The second major datum that went into this hypothesis was my personal encounter with *paranatellonta*, or *parans* as they are called. These are simultaneous bodily transits of two or more bodies over the horizon or meridian circles of a given place at the same time. However, it must be pointed out that a paran-related pair of planets does not have to be actually on the angles at a given time to be in paran. They merely have to be potentially capable of transiting the angles at that latitude at some time during the day. The fact of the matter is that with the possible exception of the Moon, because of its rapid motion in the zodiac, all bodies that are in paran will transit the angles simultaneously somewhere within the twenty-four hours of their being in an exact potential paran relationship.

I was introduced to parans through the writings of Cyril Fagan, who wrote about them in the *Primer of Sidereal Astrology*, and in various articles appearing in *American Astrology* magazine. I was personally given some more data through my good friend, A.H. Blackwell of New York. From my experience with parans, through him and through my own work, it became obvious that they were extremely important and had a significance at least equal to conventional aspects.

A brief digression is in order at this point. Parans are not simply another name for mundane squares, oppositions and conjunctions. Mundane aspects such as these refer to actual relationships in the mundane sphere at any given moment. Parans are a potential relationship that will become actual when the planets involved transit the angles. At the moment that planets in paran transit the angles, they are in a mundane aspect, but otherwise they are only in a potential mundane aspect.

There are several kinds of paran. Two planets may rise together, meaning that they are conjunct in oblique ascension under the pole of the latitude of the birthplace. Two planets may transit either the upper or lower meridian together, which corresponds to a conjunction in right ascension. Two planets may set together, which corresponds to a conjunction in oblique descension under the pole of latitude. These first three parans I refer to as conjunction parans. Now, also, one planet may rise while another sets, which corresponds to an opposition between the oblique ascension of one body and the oblique descension of the other. Or, one body may transit the upper meridian while the other transits the lower meridian, which corresponds to an opposition in right ascension. These two types of parans I refer to as opposition parans. Finally, one body may transit the meridian circle, upper or lower, while another rises or sets. These can be found whenever the right ascension of one body squares the oblique ascension or oblique descension of another. These I refer to as square parans. No other types of paran can be formed. For example, an opposition in oblique descension is not a paran, nor is one in oblique ascension. Nor can one have a paran when an oblique descension is conjunct an oblique ascension. Squares in right ascension are also not parans. Because there are only four angles to be transited, there are no paran trines or sextiles—only squares and oppositions. Another point: parans may have little resemblance to traditional aspects. Planets in a square paran may be in zodiacal trine! Planets in an opposition paran, usually oblique ascension to oblique decension, may be in zodiacal quincunx! Paran conjunctions may be several degrees wide in longitude, but exact in oblique ascension, oblique descension or right ascension.

Now to return to the main argument. I realized at once that parans were a logical outcome of Gauquelin's discoveries. If two planets have the capability of transiting two angles simultaneously, then the peaks of intensity associated with those transits by the two planets will be in phase. Thus the two diurnal rhythms of the planets will reinforce each other constructively at least at those particular transits (see figure 2). It is possible that there may even be an actual physical effect when two planets get into a constructive reinforcement pattern like this. For example, their combined physical effects might trigger an earthquake. So one of the first things that I did was to check out several earthquakes to see if parans were present. They were in all cases, usually three or four and very close, within one degree or less. Also, there were no corresponding zodiacal aspects at the same time in several cases. Now I do not consider this study to be at all conclusive, but it did whet my appetite to study this matter further.

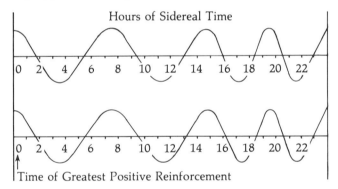

Figure 2. Diurnal Waves of Two Planets in Ascendant Paran. This illustrates the reinforcing effects that two diurnal waves have when planets are in paran. In this instance the two planets are one natal and one transiting, but the mechanism would be the same in either case. The upper planetary wave is Patty Hearst's natal Uranus as in figure 1, while the lower wave is that of the transiting Moon at the time of her kidnapping. Ascendant parans like this usually result in a fairly strong reinforcement of the waves at all four peaks; however, a square paran would tend to show reinforcement strongly at only one peak.

The final step in the process was to think in terms of transits, and then an idea occurred to me. One of the great mysteries in astrology is a concept usually called the Natal Imprint, the idea that you somehow carry your birthchart within you, so that as planets in the sky transiting through the zodiac form significant angles or aspects to the places occupied by natal planets, events occur that are symbolically related to the combined nature of the planets involved, both natal and transiting. Having just completed a book on transits and having used them as my primary predictive tool throughout my astrological career, I was quite familiar with this notion. I have found transits to be a very satisfactory tool for describing the energies that one is going to encounter in one's life, but there are certain problems. For example, the timing of an event frequently seemed to be deflected from the timing of the exact transit in the zodiac. In the introduction to my book *Planets in Transit* (Gloucester, Mass.: Para Research, Inc., 1976), I describe one way of dealing with this problem that has been quite satisfactory. But there have still been some questions. In one instance I explored the case of a woman who was run over by a train when her car stalled on the tracks. The directions, both solar arc and secondary, seemed to give satisfactory symbolism, but the transits did not. There was no way based on zodiacal transits that she could have been warned of the approaching danger. This chart is reproduced later on in this article.

In general, I have found conventional zodiacal transits to be quite unconvincing when applied to persons' deaths. It is significant to note at this point that Gauquelin also tested transits at death and found that there were no significantly frequent transits that occurred at death. These were transits taken in zodiacal measure. I, therefore, decided to try out a new type of transit on this chart, transits based on parans, i.e. relationships between transiting and natal planets such that the transiting positions are in the various types of paran with the natal planets. Because these transits are taken in oblique and right ascensions, I refer to these as "ascensional transits." These are not to be confused with the ascensional transits used in some house systems, however, in that there are no intermediate poles under which oblique ascensions may be taken. Always it is no pole, i.e. right ascension, or the pole of the latitude that is used. The results of this test were quite striking and will be shown further on. At this same time I also did a study of the time of Patty Hearst's kidnapping, an event for which the zodiacal transits are fairly unconvincing. Here again the results were dramatic, with many paran transits that were symbolically appropriate being exact to within one degree at the time of the kidnapping.

Before I proceed to an exposition of the results of these two cases, I would like to describe the new model of the Natal Imprint that emerged from this study and to describe some of its implications. It has to be pointed out that this new model came to mind before any of my case studies. The possibility of test cases showing something emerged from the model, not vice versa. Also, because of the limited number of cases that I have studied at this time, this model can in no way be said to have been proven.

We are all familiar with the diurnal rhythm of twenty-four hours. It has been amply demonstrated by scientists that there are all manner of biological clocks that correlate with the diurnal rhythm. Yet we have never given the diurnal rhythm that much attention in astrology except with regard to houses. We have not paid attention to the diurnal rhythm as a dynamic element. We have looked at the movement of the planets through the signs dynamically, that is, as cycles. Many of us have extensively studied the cycles work of Dewey and the Foundation for the Study of Cycles, trying to find correlations between those cycles and astronomical cycles. But the day cycle has always been looked at statically, as in houses. However, in this model that I am now presenting, the day cycle is the single most important cycle in that it is the carrier of energies that are modulated by the zodiacal, synodic cycles of the planets.

In the first twenty-four hours after birth, the Sun, Moon and all of the planets make a complete transit through the mundane sphere of the twelve houses. But they do not do so in phase. Depending upon the house positions of the planets, first one body will cross an angle, then another, then another. Each body goes through in that first twenty-four hours a complete four-peak intensity rhythm in the manner described above as it transits the angles. If in the natal chart any two planets hit any two angles simultaneously, there will be a constructive interference pattern between their two diurnal rhythms at that point and a paran exists.

The hypothesis is this. Each of the natal positions in the horoscope sets off a diurnal rhythm, which has its own unique phase relationship to the diurnal rhythms of the other planets depending on the mundane or house relationship of the bodies to each other. These diurnal rhythms last for the entire lifetime of an individual, much like biorhythms, forming patterns of constructive and destructive interference with the diurnal rhythms of the transiting planets. We are used to the concept of the solar day and the sidereal day, but now we are talking about a Uranian day, a Jupiterian day and so forth. At this stage of the inquiry, it is believed that the diurnal rhythms of the natal imprint are all exactly the same length as the sidereal day correlated with the angular transits of the natal positions of the planets. However, the transiting rhythms may vary according to the diurnal rate of the planet's motion in the zodiac. It is also hypothesized that the natal rhythms should always be related to the birthplace, whereas the transiting rhythms should be related to the place of the event. This leads to a very important point. Parans, depending as they do upon the latitude of the place, are latitude specific; that is, a paran will exist one moment at one latitude and not at another. Thus, ascensional transits, except those in Right Ascension, will also exist only at one latitude and not at another. One could conceivably deflect the energy of a transit by moving to a more auspicious or less auspicious latitude. It could be argued reasonably that one should always use the coordinates of the birthplace or those of the event. This matter has not been settled yet; however, the initial results have been satisfactory doing it in the manner described.

This whole approach leads to another point. If the transit signifies something due to a constructive interference pattern between a natal planet's and a transiting planet's diurnal rhythms, then one could represent transits quantitatively as waves and combine any of the natal and transiting planetary rhythms by the simple laws of wave addition. In practical terms, with the tools available to the average astrologer, this is a difficult procedure, but it would be fairly simple for a computer. If, when due to wave combination, any wave resulting from the natal and transiting diurnal waves exceeded a certain amplitude, as determined by the computer, we would know in advance that a crisis point was about to be reached and we could take precautions.

If this line of study pans out, it could provide the first reasonably reliable predictive tool that astrology has. One that could actually be used to head off accidents, illness and other undesirable phenomena. It could also be used to take advantage of favorable times for maximum results. Astrology would then fall in line with biorhythms and other rhythmic studies as a precise tool in determining timing. And if this continues to pan out, the methods for helping people determine the best time periods in their lives for various types of action would be simpler than the current methods based on complex interrelations of transits in the zodiac, progressions and even horary methods.

In conclusion, I would like to take the two examples mentioned earlier to illustrate the principle of ascensional transits in action. I should only like to point out at this time that these are not included simply because they illustrate the principles well where other cases did not. These were the two cases that I studied. Their selection was random. The only thing both cases had in common was a reasonably accurate birthchart and an accurately timed and located event chart. It is at this point that we encounter the most difficult part of this technique. Both the natal charts and the events must have specula cast for them, including in addition to longitude and latitude, right ascension, declination, oblique ascension and oblique descension for the latitude. Specula are not very hard to cast with a trigonometric calculator, but keeping track of the transits would be very difficult without a computer. To apply this technique one would need access to a computer or a reasonably sophisticated programmable calculator. For research purposes, however, many of the current computer services offer specula containing the required information. Below, the reader will see the birth chart and speculum for Patricia Hearst, and also the chart and locational speculum for her kidnapping. Also below is a tabulation of the transits, both in the zodiac and ascensional. Only major aspects in the zodiac are used, and the orb in both cases is ± 1°. I am not necessarily claiming that this is the correct orb for a transit. I am only using it to show the comparative precision of the transits in the ascensional frame of reference. Using the conjunction, sextile, square, trine and opposition for the zodiacal transits, there are eight possible ways that a transit could contact any natal factor. In ascensional transits there are ten possible ways that a transiting planet can contact a natal one. This was tabulated earlier in the paper but is repeated for convenience at the bottom of page 71. In each case the first listed coordinate is of the transiting planet while the second is the natal planet.

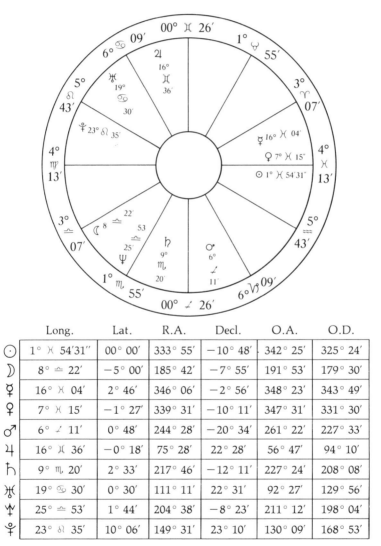

	Long.	Lat.	R.A.	Decl.	O.A.	O.D.
☉	1° ♓ 54'31"	00° 00'	333° 55'	−10° 48'	342° 25'	325° 24'
☽	8° ♎ 22'	−5° 00'	185° 42'	−7° 55'	191° 53'	179° 30'
☿	16° ♓ 04'	2° 46'	346° 06'	−2° 56'	348° 23'	343° 49'
♀	7° ♓ 15'	−1° 27'	339° 31'	−10° 11'	347° 31'	331° 30'
♂	6° ♐ 11'	0° 48'	244° 28'	−20° 34'	261° 22'	227° 33'
♃	16° ♓ 36'	−0° 18'	75° 28'	22° 28'	56° 47'	94° 10'
♄	9° ♏ 20'	2° 33'	217° 46'	−12° 11'	227° 24'	208° 08'
♅	19° ♋ 30'	0° 30'	111° 11'	22° 31'	92° 27'	129° 56'
♆	25° ♎ 53'	1° 44'	204° 38'	−8° 23'	211° 12'	198° 04'
♇	23° ♌ 35'	10° 06'	149° 31'	23° 10'	130° 09'	168° 53'

Figure 3. Patricia Hearst
February 20, 1954, 6:01 P.M. P.S.T., San Francisco, Mt. Zion Hospital

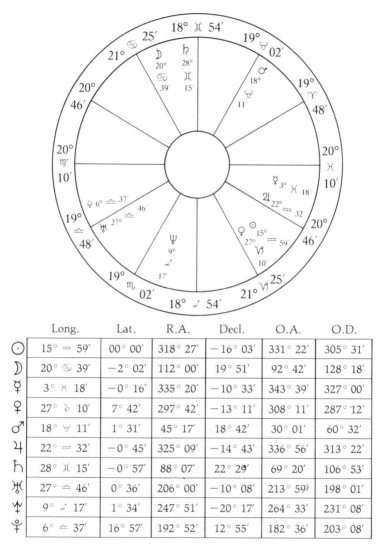

	Long.	Lat.	R.A.	Decl.	O.A.	O.D.
☉	15° ♒ 59′	00° 00′	318° 27′	−16° 03′	331° 22′	305° 31′
☽	20° ♋ 39′	−2° 02′	112° 00′	19° 51′	92° 42′	128° 18′
☿	3° ♓ 18′	−0° 16′	335° 20′	−10° 33′	343° 39′	327° 00′
♀	27° ♉ 10′	7° 42′	297° 42′	−13° 11′	308° 11′	287° 12′
♂	18° ♉ 11′	1° 31′	45° 17′	18° 42′	30° 01′	60° 32′
♃	22° ♒ 32′	−0° 45′	325° 09′	−14° 43′	336° 56′	313° 22′
♄	28° ♓ 15′	−0° 57′	88° 07′	22° 29′	69° 20′	106° 53′
♅	27° ♎ 46′	0° 36′	206° 00′	−10° 08′	213° 59′	198° 01′
♆	9° ♐ 17′	1° 34′	247° 51′	−20° 17′	264° 33′	231° 08′
♇	6° ♎ 37′	16° 57′	192° 52′	12° 55′	182° 36′	203° 08′

Figure 4. Abduction of Patricia Hearst
February 4, 1974, 21:20 P.D.T., Berkeley, California

Table of Ascensional Contacts

R.A. Con. R.A.	O.D. Opp. O.A.	R.A. Sq. O.D.
O.A. Con. O.A.	R.A. Opp. R.A.	O.A. Sq. R.A.
O.D. Con. O.D.	R.A. Sq. O.A.	O.D. Sq. R.A.
O.A. Opp. O.D.		

Obviously scanning a speculum for all of these contacts is quite a tedious procedure, which is another reason why computerization of this technique is desirable.

A tally of the transits in the two systems for Patty Hearst's abduction is most revealing. As above, the first planet listed is transiting while the second is natal. Also, after each planet is shown, one of the following letters appears: A, D, M, or I. A=rising or O.A.; D=setting or O.D.; M=culminating or R.A.; I=passing over the North Meridian or I.C., also in R.A. The orbs are also indicated with a minus sign indicating applying; plus sign, separating.

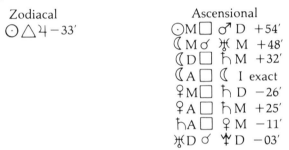

Zodiacal	Ascensional
☉△♃ −33′	☉M□ ♂D +54′
	☽M☌ ♅M +48′
	☽D□ ♄M +32′
	☽A□ ☽I exact
	♀M□ ♄D −26′
	♀A□ ♄M +25′
	♄A□ ♀M −11′
	♅D☌ ♆D −03′

The reader should be immediately struck by the greater number of close ascensional transits and the symbolic appropriateness of the ascensional transits as opposed to the one close zodiacal transit. Note also that Venus transiting is tied to the natal Saturn in two ways and that the transiting Saturn is also tied to the natal Venus. The reader is invited to check these results with the speculum. It is significant to note that there are quite a few transits that are zodiacally within a couple of degrees of being exact, but if you increase the orb in both formats the ascensional transits will increase in number even faster.

Now let us present a second case: Margaret Eden, who was killed when a train ran over her car, which had stalled on railroad tracks. The data are from my files originally garnered from an old issue of *American Astrology* magazine. Here the ascensional transits clearly show the violent nature of the event, while the zodiacal transits are quite weak. Note especially that the transiting M.C. is conjunct her natal Uranus at the time and place of the accident, both zodiacally and ascensionally. Here is the aspect tabulation.

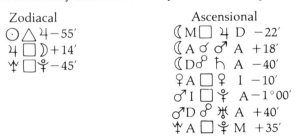

Zodiacal	Ascensional
☉△♃ −55′	☽M□ ♃D −22′
♃□☽ +14′	☽A☌ ♂A +18′
♆□☿ −45′	☽D☍ ♄A −40′
	♀A□ ♀I −10′
	♂I□ ☿A −1°00′
	♂D☍ ♅A +40′
	♆A□ ☿M +35′

First of all, note the symbolic appropriateness of the ascensional transits, especially the Mars-Pluto and Mars-Uranus interactions. Note also that the only really symbolically appropriate zodiacal transit, Neptune square Pluto, is also effective in the ascensional system.

These are only two examples, but they are typical of the results that I have been getting. I am beginning to wonder what would have been the results of Gauquelin's transit tests if he had done them in this manner. Obviously some kind of rigorous statistical test is in order to determine if this effect is real or only apparent, like so many astrological indications.

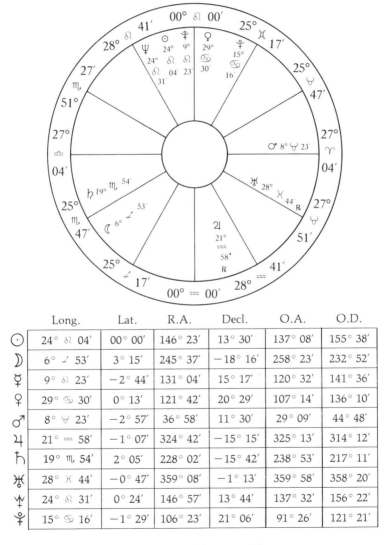

	Long.	Lat.	R.A.	Decl.	O.A.	O.D.
☉	24° ♌ 04′	00° 00′	146° 23′	13° 30′	137° 08′	155° 38′
☽	6° ♐ 53′	3° 15′	245° 37′	−18° 16′	258° 23′	232° 52′
☿	9° ♌ 23′	−2° 44′	131° 04′	15° 17′	120° 32′	141° 36′
♀	29° ♋ 30′	0° 13′	121° 42′	20° 29′	107° 14′	136° 10′
♂	8° ♉ 23′	−2° 57′	36° 58′	11° 30′	29° 09′	44° 48′
♃	21° ♒ 58′	−1° 07′	324° 42′	−15° 15′	325° 13′	314° 12′
♄	19° ♏ 54′	2° 05′	228° 02′	−15° 42′	238° 53′	217° 11′
♅	28° ♓ 44′	−0° 47′	359° 08′	−1° 13′	359° 58′	358° 20′
♆	24° ♌ 31′	0° 24′	146° 57′	13° 44′	137° 32′	156° 22′
♇	15° ♋ 16′	−1° 29′	106° 23′	21° 06′	91° 26′	121° 21′

Figure 5. Margaret Eden
August 17, 1926, 10:20 A.M. P.S.T., Long Beach, California

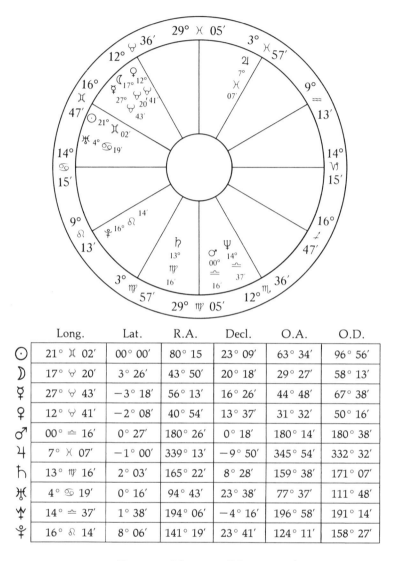

Figure 6. Margaret Eden's Death
June 12, 1950, 7:27 A.M. P.D.T., Fullerton, California

	Long.	Lat.	R.A.	Decl.	O.A.	O.D.
☉	21° ♓ 02′	00° 00′	80° 15	23° 09′	63° 34′	96° 56′
☽	17° ♉ 20′	3° 26′	43° 50′	20° 18′	29° 27′	58° 13′
☿	27° ♉ 43′	−3° 18′	56° 13′	16° 26′	44° 48′	67° 38′
♀	12° ♉ 41′	−2° 08′	40° 54′	13° 37′	31° 32′	50° 16′
♂	00° ♎ 16′	0° 27′	180° 26′	0° 18′	180° 14′	180° 38′
♃	7° ♓ 07′	−1° 00′	339° 13′	−9° 50′	345° 54′	332° 32′
♄	13° ♍ 16′	2° 03′	165° 22′	8° 28′	159° 38′	171° 07′
♅	4° ♋ 19′	0° 16′	94° 43′	23° 38′	77° 37′	111° 48′
♆	14° ♎ 37′	1° 38′	194° 06′	−4° 16′	196° 58′	191° 14′
♇	16° ♌ 14′	8° 06′	141° 19′	23° 41′	124° 11′	158° 27′

I am not suggesting that zodiacal aspects and conventional transits are worthless. It is too soon in this inquiry to say anything yet. I suspect that what is happening here is that the zodiacal rhythms are long-period waves which become superimposed upon the diurnal waves, much as in AM radio, where waves corresponding to the sounds of the radio broadcast are superimposed upon the energy of the carrier frequency, the frequency of the particular radio station. The actual energy is due to the radio-station frequency, but the data is communicated by the modulations of amplitude.

Similarly, the diurnal rhythms carry the energy, but the information is conveyed to the human brain by the long-term zodiacal rhythms superimposed upon the diurnal. Thus, natal delineation should be handled by a combination of zodiacal aspects and parans, while transits should be taken primarily in the various ascensions.

Again, I wish to make it clear to the reader that I am not under the delusion that I have proved anything in this simple and limited study, but I am hoping that others will join me in this line of research so that something useful may come out of it.

Postscript—August, 1982

Since writing the original article, I have begun to employ a different method for looking at the transiting and natal parans. The main points of this paper, however, are unchanged. In the original paper, a planet's right ascension, oblique ascension and descension were given in the tables along with longitude, latitude and declination. In these tables one has to look for several types of paran and to recognize significant angles between various R.A.'s, O.A.'s and O.D.'s. Here is a summary of what was described.

O.A. Conjunct O.A.	Two bodies rise together.
O.A. Opposition O.D.	One rises while the other sets.
O.A. Square R.A.	One rises, the other culminates or anti-culminates.
O.D. Conjunct O.D.	Two bodies set together.
O.D. Square R.A.	One body sets, the other culminates or anti-culminates.
R.A. Conjunct R.A.	Two bodies culminate and anti-culminate together.
R.A. Opposition R.A.	One culminates while the other anti-culminates.

As in the text all other combinations are meaningless.

These combinations are somewhat difficult to see in the tables, especially as the values are given in 360-degree notation. One has to do a great deal of mental juggling in order to get everything to come out correctly. Since I wrote this article I have discovered the much simpler method of representation that I now describe. Arthur Blackwell and Gary Duncan both have contributed to my understanding.

Instead of representing the planetary positions in R.A., O.A. and O.D., the new method is to compute the right ascension of the midheaven (R.A.M.C.) of the times when the planets' positions would cross the four angles of the chart. The reader must remember that at the time of any event, astronomical or astrological, there is some degree on the equator going over the M.C. Most astrologers use sidereal time to represent this. The R.A.M.C. is simply the sidereal time multiplied by 15 to convert hours, minutes and seconds into degrees, minutes and seconds. R.A.M.C. is simply another way of stating times. I prefer to use degrees rather than hours because the orbs are more obvious. I, like most astrologers, am more comfortable with arc measure than time measure. However, one could present these values either as arc or as time.

The rationale is simple. If the R.A.M.C. at the time of a body's rising is the same as (or within acceptable orb of) the R.A.M.C. of another body's culminating, then we have a square paran between the two bodies. The elegant part of this mode of representation is that we do not have to find a square between the O.A. of the first body and the R.A. of the second body. We merely have to look for a *conjunction* between the R.A.M.C.'s of the two events. To use this method, make a table similar to the ones in this article. For each planet give the R.A.M.C. of rising, the R.A.M.C. of culminating, the R.A.M.C. of setting and the R.A.M.C. of anti-culminating. These four R.A.M.C.'s can be derived from the R.A., O.A. and O.D. of each planet by the following formulas.

R.A.M.C. of rising	O.A. − 90 degrees
R.A.M.C. of culminating	R.A. unchanged
R.A.M.C. of setting	O.D. + 90 degrees
R.A.M.C. of anti-culm.	R.A. + 180 degrees

Of course, whenever values go below 0 or above 360 you should add or subtact 360 degrees as appropriate. Below are the tables for Patricia Hearst and Margaret Eden, giving the planetary positions as revised according to this method. The longitudes, latitudes and declinations are as in the original tables and are not repeated here.

If any R.A.M.C. of the natal chart is conjunct any R.A.M.C. of the event chart, then an ascensional transit is taking place. If Rising is conjunct Rising then there is a rising conjunction paran; if Rising is conjunct Setting then there is an opposition paran along the horizon; if Setting is conjunct Setting, there is a setting conjunction paran and so forth. You need only be concerned with conjunctions of R.A.M.C.'s. Aside from this methodological change, there are no changes in the basic observations of this paper.

Patricia Hearst Natal Chart

R.A.M.C.'s of

	Rising	Culminating	Setting	Anti-Culminating
Sun	252 25	333 55	55 24	153 55
Moon	101 53	185 42	269 30	5 42
Mercury	258 23	346 06	73 49	166 06
Venus	257 31	339 31	61 30	159 31
Mars	171 22	244 28	317 33	64 28
Jupiter	326 47	75 28	184 10	255 28
Saturn	137 24	217 46	298 08	37 46
Uranus	2 27	111 11	219 56	291 11
Neptune	121 12	204 38	288 04	24 38
Pluto	40 09	149 31	258 53	329 31

R.A.M.C. of Chart = 58 17

Abduction of Patricia Hearst

R.A.M.C.'s of

	Rising	Culminating	Setting	Anti-Culminating
Sun	241 22	318 27	35 31	138 27
Moon	5 42	112 00	218 18	292 00
Mercury	253 39	335 20	57 00	155 20
Venus	218 11	297 42	17 12	117 42
Mars	300 01	45 17	150 32	225 17
Jupiter	246 56	325 09	43 22	145 09
Saturn	339 20	88 07	196 53	268 07
Uranus	123 59	206 00	288 01	26 00
Neptune	174 33	247 51	321 08	67 51
Pluto	92 35	192 52	293 08	12 52

R.A.M.C. of Chart = 77 40

Margaret Eden Natal Chart

R.A.M.C.'s of

	Rising	Culminating	Setting	Anti-Culminating
Sun	47 08	146 23	245 38	326 23
Moon	168 23	245 37	322 52	65 37
Mercury	30 32	131 04	231 36	311 04
Venus	17 14	121 42	226 10	301 42
Mars	299 09	36 58	134 48	216 58
Jupiter	245 13	324 42	44 12	144 42
Saturn	148 53	228 02	307 11	48 02
Uranus	269 58	359 09	88 20	179 09
Neptune	47 32	146 57	246 22	326 57
Pluto	1 26	106 23	211 21	286 23

R.A.M.C. of Chart = 122 11

Margaret Eden's Death

R.A.M.C.'s of

	Rising	Culminating	Setting	Anti-Culminating
Sun	333 34	80 15	186 56	260 15
Moon	299 27	43 50	148 13	223 50
Mercury	314 48	56 13	157 38	236 13
Venus	301 32	40 54	140 16	220 54
Mars	90 14	180 26	270 38	0 26
Jupiter	255 54	339 13	62 32	159 13
Saturn	69 38	165 22	261 07	345 22
Uranus	347 37	94 43	201 48	274 43
Neptune	106 58	194 06	281 14	14 06
Pluto	34 11	141 19	248 27	321 19

R.A.M.C. of Chart = 359 10

8

Crises of Human Growth

There are rhythms in human development, rhythms that weave in and out of each other, sometimes working together to reinforce each other, sometimes working against each other. Astrologers have long known about these rhythms, for that is the central study of astrology: the relation between the rhythms of human development and cycles of the heavens. *Astrology is nothing more than this*. It is not an effort to chart Fate or to describe an individual's immutable destiny. Astrology teaches that every individual is a creature of the cosmos and reflects its cycles. These cycles in turn affect the probabilities of different kinds of experience happening within an individual's life at various times.

At times, life cycles work concurrently to bring about periods of crisis in an individual's development, times when structures that are thought to be safe, reliable and supportive of one's existence either cease to support one's life and crumble away altogether or become a threat to the well-being and happiness of the individual. In either case, *change becomes inevitable* as the individual is forced to create a new life with new structure in order to make more room in life for living.

Although a crisis may be more terrifying than gratifying, its principal characteristic is the opportunity for more freedom. What we do at such a time will have a greater effect upon our futures than what we do at another time. The past releases its hold upon us so that a new direction may be chosen.

Psychologists have begun to notice that adulthood is not static. The older view that most psychological development takes place in early childhood is being replaced with the idea that life is continuous development, and that for life to assume a static, persistent form in adulthood is more an aberration than a pattern of normality. Psychologists also have begun to recognize that there are patterns of crisis in adulthood that are common to most people although, of course, they vary considerably from person to person. And, obviously, there are also crises that are peculiar to the individual's own development.

Astrology has also been aware of this, but for much longer. While its philosophy has changed from era to era, astrology's primary purpose has always been to discover not only who and what a person is but also to determine when a person will encounter crises. The astrology of the past strove to determine crises in terms of *particular events*, whereas modern astrology looks at an individual life more in terms of the *whole person*, the psychological nature as well as the kinds of circumstances that such a nature might attract.

Astrology shows that general life crises—that is, ones that tend to occur at specific ages in large numbers of people, as opposed to personal crises peculiar to the circumstances and dynamics of one's own life—are signified by the transits of the outer planets to their own natal positions, forming what are often called "hard aspects." These are the aspects derived from dividing the circle by 1, 2, 4, 8, etc., giving rise to the angles 360° or 0° (the conjunction), 180° (the opposition), 90° (the square), 45° (the semisquare) and 135° (the sesquiquadrate). For the purposes of this discussion the semisquare and the sesquiquadrate will not be discussed, as they represent less severe critical periods. The inner-planet transits are not deemed significant because they do not represent long-term trends.

However, because the outer planets, with the exception of Pluto, move through the chart at about the same rate of speed for all individuals, they will form critical aspects to themselves at about the same point in life for every individual. Thus, in contrast to outer-planet transits to bodies other than themselves, which give rise to crisis patterns that distinguish individuals from each other, outer-planet transits to their own natal positions will indicate a pattern that everyone shares in common—admittedly, however, not to the same degree. Everyone will have the transiting Saturn conjoin natal Saturn between the ages of twenty-eight and thirty, for example. It is these transits which give rise to the general pattern of life crises that are to be seen throughout the population.

Some of these crises are more important than others. The most important crises are those indicated by "returns," i.e., the transit of a planet over its natal position by conjunction. There are two of these which most people encounter: the transits of Saturn over itself at ages twenty-nine and fifty-eight approximately. Many people also live long enough to encounter the Uranus return at eighty-four.

A second type of important crisis arises because of the relation between the cycles of the outer planets such that three-quarters of a Saturn cycle of twenty-nine years, i.e. twenty-one years, also equals one-quarter of the Uranus cycle of eighty-four years, which is twenty-one years. Also one-half of the Uranus cycle of eighty-four years, forty-two years, is close to one-quarter of a Neptune cycle of one hundred sixty-five years, i.e. forty-one years. These planetary-cycle relationships cause crises to come in groups at times, which makes these crises particularly intense.

In general, crises signified by a single opposition or square are less significant, unless they coincide with another crisis signified by an outer planet transiting a body other than itself. It is the relationship of the general-crisis transits (planets to their own positions) to the individual-crisis transits (planets transiting other planets) that determines the severity of life crises. Jupiter will not be discussed in this connection because, for some reason, it does not seem to be as significant a timer of major crises as the planets from Saturn out.

Table of Cycle Lengths

	Full Cycle	Half Cycle	Quarter Cycle
Saturn	29.46 yrs.	14.73 yrs.	7.36 yrs.
Uranus	84.02 yrs.	42.01 yrs.	21.00 yrs.
Neptune	164.80 yrs.	82.40 yrs.	41.20 yrs.
Pluto	247.08 yrs.	123.54 yrs.	61.77 yrs.

Although the transits by semisquare and sesquiquadrate have been mentioned as crisis angles, these crises, too, will be omitted. Although they are qualitatively similar to transits by square, they are usually much less intense. Several simultaneous transits by semisquare and sesquiquadrate, however, can be quite significant.

First Saturn Square

The first crisis that we shall consider—the square at seven years of age—is important simply because it is the first general-crisis transit. It signifies the transition from early childhood to later childhood and eventual adolescence. It also signifies the increasing role of discipline and the need to conform to other people's expectations. The child is typically expected to be less spontaneous and more orderly in his or her behavior. How a child handles this crisis and the other pressures that the child experiences at this time can make the difference between an adult who knows how to be an individual, true to his or her own self, and one who does not, but lives strictly according to other people's expectations. This crisis typically manifests as discipline problems and difficulties between the child and parents, as well as any other group of people who are involved in teaching the child discipline. Obviously school can be a problem.

First Saturn Opposition

This occurs at fourteen years of age, and its significance varies from culture to culture. It is significant that many older cultures initiated children into adulthood at about this age. The Jewish Bar Mitzvah at thirteen is a survival into modern times of this custom. But in our culture it signifies the transition from childhood into adolescence, that peculiar period when the individual has a more or less adult body and emotional needs but is held in "suspended animation" until society judges that he or she is mature enough to play an adult role. It is curious that, until quite recently, the next Saturn crisis at twenty-one years of age was the time when individuals were allowed to assume adult roles. Yet, although legal majority occurs at eighteen or nineteen, many people do not expect an individual to behave as an adult until twenty-nine, when Saturn makes its first return. Societies seem to settle upon one or another Saturn-crisis age for recognizing their children as adults.

The turbulent nature of adolescence is too well known to go into here, but there are some things about this transit that are worth saying from the vantage point of astrological symbolism. This transit is the opposition phase of the first Saturn cycle and therefore, like all opposition transits, it represents a culmination. In this case it is the culmination of biological growth. In every cycle, the first 180° from conjunction to opposition is the period of physical development. The first fourteen years of life see most of the actual biological and, for that matter, psychological growth of a human being. While we recognize that there is much maturing left to go, the basic apparatus of the body and mind are fully developed. It is simply that the adolescent hasn't learned how to use it yet. One current leader in the human potential movement has defined an adolescent as "an adult who hasn't gotten his act together." The second 180° of any cycle represents a time in which the entity that has come to be in the first 180° of the cycle seeks a purpose for itself and attempts to integrate itself into a larger context. Therefore, the second fourteen years of the first Saturn cycle concentrate on the integration of the maturing individual into a social context, in which he or she must learn the give and take of adult life and the nature of his or her strengths and limitations in a social context. The Saturn crisis of twenty to twenty-one represents a critical phase in that development.

The Twenty to Twenty-one Year Crisis

At this age there are two transits that occur nearly simultaneously. How close they fall together depends on where the individual is born in the Sun-Saturn and Sun-Uranus annual cycles. These are the transits of Saturn square to natal Saturn moving toward the return conjunction, and Uranus square natal Uranus moving toward the opposition.

The Saturn square Saturn, as mentioned in the previous section, is a crisis concerning social integration and the fulfillment of the social obligations and expectations. The Uranus square Uranus is a crisis that challenges the individual to continually renew his or her life structures so that they remain supportive instead of restrictive. If these two issues are in conflict, as they are to some extent in most people's lives, then this will be a period of tension during which the individual must make a choice between the following two questions: "Do I do what is socially expected of me, fully assume the role of an adult with a complete set of responsibilities and, to some extent, deny my inner need for continued growth and experimentation? Or do I rebel against the forces that seek to limit me, go off and do whatever I need in order to find myself and build a life structure that is uniquely mine and that works for me no matter how different it is from those around me?"

The decision that is made at this point depends on a number of factors symbolized by other components in the chart. These are too complex to go into here, but the choice has a great effect upon what happens in the immediate future and reaches its crisis during the Saturn return at twenty-nine.

Four Life-Scripts for the Twenties

There are basically four patterns that can be followed after the Saturn and Uranus crises of twenty to twenty-one. These are simply derived from whether one chooses the first or second path as outlined above, and whether one handles either of these choices well or poorly.

The first case represents one who has chosen to take on a fully adult role after twenty-one, then cultivates a career or other life-role and becomes a member of some kind of community. Let us assume that the choice was a good one and that the individual in question fits into the chosen role without doing violence to his or her inner nature. In this case, the twenties will be spent learning the ropes of the chosen path, whether it be a career, a family or whatever. For this person there are no serious problems in the immediate future.

The second case is represented by one who makes the same choice in conflict with his or her inner nature. This is usually the result of following others' expectations rather than one's own needs and desires. For this person there will usually be a serious effort to make the grade but, as thirty approaches, the level of restlessness and dissatisfaction will increase considerably. There is the feeling that youth has been wasted and all that remains is the dull, gray experience of an adulthood that came too soon. Both sexes make this mistake. But women, with the pressure to get married and raise a family regardless of their own inner aspirations, are somewhat more inclined to run into these problems. For these people of either sex, there will be a serious crisis at twenty-nine.

The third pattern occurs in those who have chosen the Uranian path—not to settle down into a sociably acceptable lifestyle, but instead to go out into the world and find their own unique and personally tailored mode of living. For most of these people, the search will last nearly all of the years from twenty-one to twenty-nine. Otherwise, they will have no serious problems.

Problems again occur in the fourth instance—those who also choose the Uranian path but do not find themselves or their life-direction. These are often people who have no one clearly defined goal, such as a particular career or task. Their life-direction does not involve a specific purpose, but revolves instead around learning certain kinds of lessons and having particular experiences. For these persons the crisis at twenty-nine can be extremely difficult.

The Saturn Return of Twenty-eight to Twenty-nine

This is among the more significant of the life-crises. It is the end of the beginning, although many people on the verge of thirty feel that it is more like the beginning of the end. During this time one often feels older than one will again feel for many years. There is a sense of urgency, a sense that youth is departing and there are many things left to be done that can only be done while one is young. This feeling is, to quite an extent, illusory. There is really much more time than it seems. However, the reality behind the feeling is that this is a time in which one should get one's life together and set about being useful. No matter which life-script was followed in the twenties, this is a period in which all factors extraneous to the pursuit of one's true calling are to be eliminated. If one is off the proper lifetrack, then one should get onto it. Often events will force this in some way. This is one of those times in which a person should allow whatever seems to be passing out of his or her life to pass out without resistance. Whatever it might be, it has fulfilled its function and should be released. It is extremely important to do this, because if one holds on and resists the energies moving toward change, one may be successful at doing so. But it is a case of winning the battle and losing the war because, as age comes, it becomes clearer that life is structured in a way that is deadening, not vivifying. Life thus becomes extremely empty and meaningless. At the second Saturn return at fifty-eight to fifty-nine there is sometimes a second chance, but it is much harder to alter set patterns at this time. For those who resist the energies of the first Saturn return, the second can be quite difficult.

Each of the four different life-scripts of the twenties that were discussed above involves different reactions to the Saturn return. The first two types who chose the socially acceptable path at twenty-one will react differently depending upon whether the choice was appropriate or not. The first group will settle down into their patterns quite comfortably and begin to win recognition for what they are doing. For these people this time may be the beginning of real success in life. The second type will often realize that the choice was terribly wrong and go through a series of changes that will result in a more appropriate life-direction—more appropriate, that is, in terms of real inner needs as opposed to the expectations of others. In fact, many of these people will make changes in their lives which seem quite outrageous to their contemporaries. They will abandon apparently good jobs and marriages, and will often look like their younger contemporaries of twenty-one who have taken the Uranian path, although they do so less light-heartedly and with considerably grimmer determination to make it all work out.

Those who chose the Uranian paths also vary in their reactions to the Saturn return. Those who have really been finding themselves in the intervening years will feel that the time has come to do something real and significant, and will settle into something that fits who and what they are. Those who have not found themselves at all, or who have not defined their life-directions even for the present, will often be quite upset about the passage of time and will feel very urgently pressed. The danger is that these people will lose respect for themselves because they remain the only "rolling stones" among their contemporaries, or that they will make an arbitrary decision and become involved in something that is not right for them even in the short run. These are the people who will have the greatest difficulty as time goes by.

The First Saturn Square of the Second Cycle

The chief function of this transit is to test the validity of the choices made at the Saturn return. This is not one of the more serious crises, but adjustments are often made at this time that help the paths taken during the return period serve one's life more effectively. Often this transit comes close to the third Jupiter return, and Jupiter transits often temper Saturn transits. Even so, people should look to their lives very carefully during this transit and make whatever changes are necessary.

The Midlife-Crisis Transits

Between the ages of thirty-nine and forty-three, there occurs the most concentrated string of crisis transits of any point in life. In this short span of time, Uranus opposes Uranus, Saturn opposes Saturn and Neptune squares Neptune. Each of these independently would be fairly intense, but the combination makes this one of the most turbulent periods of life—especially since *popular opinion assumes that one should be beyond extreme turbulence by this age* and settled down into a comfortable routine. Thus, it is a great surprise to everyone when middle-aged men and women suddenly leave old marriages or jobs, or when the settled housewife begins to demand independence from her family to go out and find a career, or when the responsible father of a family suddenly abandons it and takes up with a girl half his age. Not that this happens to everybody, of course, but everyone is forced to make *some* readjustments.

The transit that most sets the tone for this period is the opposition between transiting Uranus and natal Uranus, which occurs between the ages of thirty-nine and forty-two. Like all oppositions, this one signifies a change of orientation, and, because Uranus is especially related to changes of a particular kind, this is an extremely important set of changes.

The most interesting change is that of *polarity reversal*. Uranus represents situations in which a thing will change suddenly into its opposite without going through an intermediate state. Male may suddenly become female, left move to right, good become evil and so forth. In human life this is the time—as much because of Neptune as Uranus—when one must begin to deal with the issue of death, not because it is close by, but because one has reached (in conventional terms at least) the peak of life (more mental than physical), and one's accomplishments seem jeopardized by the fact of eventual death. The most important thing now is to attain inner peace, inner solidity and "grace under pressure." The realization comes that the material circumstances of life cannot provide these in the long run. Perspectives shift; what was once important becomes less so and vice-versa.

Another polarity shift, aside from outer to inner or life to death, occurs in sexual role-identities. It has been observed by researchers (see Gail Sheehy, *Passages*) that males who have been primarily involved in career, advancement and achievement now become more concerned with relationships, with being loved and loving, with the softer and gentler aspects of life—in other words, with things that are usually thought of as more feminine than masculine. Meanwhile, women who have been involved primarily with their homes and families, content to experience much of life through their husbands, suddenly become impatient with their passivity and desire to go out into the world and experience on their own, achieve on their own, and become involved in careers and jobs. Correspondingly, career or working women become more concerned with a home, marriage and family. In short, where a personality has been "male," it becomes more "female," and vice-versa, regardless of one's sex. The individual psyche is trying to become whole by expressing other aspects of the self that have not been adequately expressed previously. This phenomenon is one of the major contributing factors to marital instability during this time. Just as the male begins to understand and become concerned about many of the issues that the female has always been concerned about, the female begins to answer a need to become something more than a satellite of her husband. This assumes, of course, that the marriage has been structured more or less along traditional lines.

The Saturn-Saturn opposition that occurs at about this same time makes matters a bit more complicated. Fundamentally, it represents the culmination of the processes begun at the Saturn return of twenty-eight to twenty-nine. It may be a culmination of a career choice or a cycle of psychological development. But whatever it may be, it is, like the Uranus-Uranus opposition that occurs at the same time, a change of polarity. Here, too, the shift is from succeeding at creating something to finding out what that something may be for, what significance it may have, and what it really means for the individual. The by-products of bad choices made at the Saturn return may completely fall apart at this time.

Saturn also has to do with one's belief systems. Therefore, there is also, at this time, a crisis involving one's views about the nature of reality and the world one lives in—a crisis made all the more likely by the presence of Neptune square Neptune. Neptune challenges one's entire reality structure just at the time that structure is undergoing a critical period in terms of the Saturn cycle.

The exact set of issues that have to be confronted at the midlife crisis period vary from individual to individual and cannot be generally described for all persons. Yet it is clear from what has already been said that this is one of the most intensely critical periods one can face. As the boundary line between building up one's life in material terms and, one would hope, making one's life meaningful in spiritual terms, it is very important that this time be handled well. It often is not.

The most common difficulty that people have with this crisis is trying to hold on to what they had in the previous period. Usually this consists of denying one's age and attempting to look and act younger. Society tries very hard to make people follow this route as well. It is extremely flattering for fifty-year-olds to be told that they look and act young for their age. From an astrological point of view, this is a sign of impending maladjustment to the circumstances of life.

The problem is that we tend to think of growing old as a process of ossification, of decay. There is little recognition of the spiritual side of growing older, or of the potential wisdom of age. It is the frantic effort to stay young and to hold on desperately to the past that actually creates the rigidity of age. To put it simply, it is the resistance to aging that ages one most rapidly.

The Square of Pluto to Pluto

This square represents a very significant crisis period, and it is the only one that strikes different age groups at different points in time. Because Pluto varies in its orbital speed considerably, this transit may occur anywhere between the early forties and the late sixties. At present, it is affecting persons of about fifty years of age. Since Pluto is now speeding up, it will occur earlier and earlier in people's lives until those born in the early 1950s will face this square in their forties as part of the midlife crisis!

This transit represents a crisis in the ability of people to handle major transformations and power shifts in their lives. Jimmy Carter was elected president under this transit, but also had the difficulties with Bert Lance at the end of it. The Watergate break-in occurred exactly at the time Nixon was having his first transit, and the transit continued throughout the "leakage" of the Watergate affair. But Nixon was also reelected by a large margin during this transit. An individual whom I know was offered a job as head of his department under this transit, but didn't want it. Another person I know is having a major crisis during this transit because he is reluctant to take over a family business that his son is running badly. One may be exalted or brought down by this transit. The sole determining factor is *one's ability to deal with power creatively*.

Later Crises

There are other critical periods as one gets older, but none has quite the impact of those occurring earlier in life. The major ones are the second Saturn return, the closing Uranus to Uranus square and, for some, the Uranus return and the Neptune-Neptune opposition in one's eighties.

The second Saturn return and the closing Uranus-Uranus square occur a couple of years apart in the late fifties and early sixties, but not quite close enough to strongly reinforce each other. The second Saturn return at fifty-eight to fifty-nine is not too difficult, unless one did not deal well with the first return. If such is the case, then one is in the unenviable position of having to break free, rather late in life, of old patterns and establish a new and more appropriate life-direction.

The closing Uranus square can represent many of the same issues as the second Saturn return. It can also represent a crisis in one's spiritual and psychological adjustment to age. This is a particularly bad time to cling to one's youth.

The Uranus return and the Neptune-Neptune opposition happen to too few people for generalizations to be made. But it is quite safe to say that even at this age one can encounter significant crises of development and that sweeping changes can occur. That major life crises can occur at an age at which most people think life is over proves that life is not over until the moment of death. One must always remain flexible because growth never stops, and there is always something positive to do at any given time. Aging is not a negative process.

9

Astrology's Second Dimension: Declination and Latitude

In looking at the typical horoscope one could conclude that the solar system is entirely flat with all of the planets revolving around the Sun in a single plane. While in the case of most planets this is approximately true, in the case of some planets it is *not* true, and in the case of the fixed stars not even approximately true. And even in those cases where we are dealing with bodies that are approximately in the same plane, there are surprising consequences to be encountered when the solar system and the fixed stars are not treated as if they were all in one plane. This article will deal with these consequences. However, it is incumbent on me to warn the reader that many of the questions that I will raise will not be answered! Much research will be necessary before many of these questions can be answered. But let me assure you that these questions do not affect only difficult and obscure aspects of the art of astrology. Some of astrology's most fundamental and everyday methods are called into question.

Some Basics

While the bulk of this article will not use technical and mathematical language, some basic points about measuring positions in space do have to be made. We will take this as slowly and easily as possible, in order that the non-technical reader will be able to follow.

As most readers are probably aware, objects in space are referred to by the use of three dimensions. If one were precisely to locate an object in a room, one might describe the object as being four feet off the floor, two feet forward from the rear wall, and seven feet away from the left-hand wall.

These three numbers, four, two and seven, plus the notation as to which walls they are being measured from, locate the object unambiguously in the space of the room. Walls in a typical room are at right angles to each other. Whenever *points in space* are located as if they were being measured from the nearest "walls," this is called a *rectangular coordinate system*. Usually one "wall" is designated as the X coordinate, another as the Y coordinate, and the last as the Z coordinate. Of course, walls are not actually used for reference in mathematics, but planes or plane surfaces are used in much the same way as we have described.

In astrology, however, rectangular coordinates are not used extensively. Astrology uses angles measured in degrees to locate objects in space. But like the rectangular coordinate system, astrology must *also use three numbers to locate a point in space completely*. Most astrologers are only aware of *one* of these numbers. Here is how the astrological system works.

The system used in astrology is called a *polar coordinate system*, or a spherical coordinate system. These two terms are equivalent. What we do to locate something is first to define a reference plane. The reference plane is a plane surface along which we will measure angles. The horizon is a possible reference plane, for example. Let us use the horizon in the discussion that follows. Along the reference plane, in this case the horizon, we take one direction and designate it as zero degrees. On the horizon we might take the direction, due east, as our zero degree direction.

Now let us assume that we are standing in an open field with an unlimited view of the horizon, and we wish to describe the location of a windmill that we see in the distance. We take our right arm, point it to the east direction, and then turn it parallel to the horizon east to west, or clockwise, until we are pointing at the base of the windmill. With some kind of measuring device we measure the number of degrees through which we have turned our arm, let us say 120 degrees from due east. Now we raise our arm until it is pointing at the top of the windmill, and again we measure the angle through which we have raised our arm, say 15 degrees from horizontal. Now we look at the windmill and with another measuring instrument we measure its distance away from us, say 300 ft. The three measurements, 120 degrees along the horizon, 15 degrees up from the horizon and 300 feet away in distance are the three coordinates that establish the location of the top of the windmill with respect to ourselves.

Of these three coordinates, the 120 degrees is called a horizontal or longitudinal coordinate, or longitude for short. The 15 degrees is called a vertical, or latitudinal coordinate, or latitude for short. The 300 foot distance is called simply the distance, but in astronomy is called the *radius vector*. Every polar coordinate measurement has a longitude, a latitude and a radius vector, although different polar coordinate systems with different reference planes may have special names for the longitude, latitude and radius vector peculiar to that system. Let's look briefly at three systems encountered in astrology.

Geographic Coordinates

This is the system used to locate objects on the Earth's surface. The reference plane is the geographic equator. The zero direction is established by a north-south great circle passing through Greenwich, England. The horizontal coordinate or longitude is called geographic longitude. It is measured both east (counterclockwise as viewed from the north geographic pole) and west (clockwise as viewed from the north pole.) The vertical coordinate or latitude is called geographic latitude. The radius vector in this system is not very important, and has no special name. It is simply the distance from the center of the Earth.

Ecliptical Coordinate System

This is the system that is most important in astrology. Its reference plane is the plane of the ecliptic. The ecliptic is the plane in which the Sun appears to revolve around the Earth, but in fact it is the plane in which the Earth revolves around the Sun. The ecliptic is also the central plane of the zodiac. The zero direction of the ecliptical system is the point where the Sun appears to be each year at the exact beginning of Spring in the northern hemisphere. It is called the vernal point, vernal equinox, or simply zero Aries. Bodies in space are located by taking counterclockwise measurements along the ecliptic from zero Aries until one is pointing directly under or over the body. *This is the horizontal coordinate or longitude and it is called, using the full term, celestial longitude. The vertical coordinate or latitude is called celestial latitude.*

An upward latitude measurement is called north or positive latitude. A downward latitude measurement is called south or negative latitude. The distance coordinate is called the radius vector. Of these three dimensions astrologers use mostly the first, celestial longitude, simply calling it longitude. Celestial latitude, or simply latitude, is used hardly at all. Radius vectors are used even less, although in the printouts from some of the major computer services there are listed values called distance values, which are derived from the radius vectors of the planets. As we will see, *consideration of the latitudes of bodies may be extremely important*, although not exactly in ways that might be obvious at first glance.

Equatorial System

This system is very closely related to the system of geographical coordinates used on the Earth's surface. It is used, however, to locate the positions of bodies in space rather than on the Earth's surface. There are in fact two celestial equatorial systems in use that concern astrology.

Both of these systems use the plane of the Earth's equator as the reference plane, that is, all angles are first measured parallel to it. However, the more commonly used of these two systems, in astrology at least, uses the same zero

Aries direction as the zero line in the ecliptical system. In fact zero Aries is one of the two directions (the other being zero Libra) along which *the celestial equator and the ecliptic coincide.* So both the ecliptical and this equatorial system use the same zero direction line. However, when one measures along the celestial equator instead of the ecliptic, the horizontal coordinate or longitude is called *right ascension.* Right ascension, or R.A. for short, is also measured counterclockwise from zero Aries.

The other equatorial system uses the point of the equator that is exactly due south of the observer at a particular spot on the earth as the zero direction line. Then angles are measured clockwise along the equator instead of counterclockwise. This measurement is called the *hour angle* of the body. Whereas the right ascension of a body is the same for any observer on Earth, because it uses a celestial point, zero Aries, as its zero direction line, an hour angle of a body is different for every observer on Earth because it uses a local direction, south, to establish a zero line. Both right ascension and hour angles are often measured in hours, minutes and seconds instead of degrees, minutes and seconds. An hour equals 15 degrees, a time minute equals 15 arc minutes, and a time second equals 15 arc seconds. There are, of course, 24 hours in the circle of 360 degrees. A zodiacal sign of 30 degrees and the ideal house are both two hours long.

Hour angles may seem very foreign to astrology, but they are not. The hour angle between the local south point of the equator and the zero Aries direction line is the local sidereal time. Clock-time is derived by a circuitous process from the hour angle of the Sun. One could conceivably have a lunar time based upon the hour angle of the Moon, or a time for any planet based upon the hour angle of that particular planet. Hour angles are important because they define time.

The vertical coordinate of both equatorial systems is the same. It is called *declination.* Measurement in an upward direction is called north declination or positive declination, while downward measurement is called south or negative declination. The distance coordinate in both equatorial systems is the same radius vector that we encountered with the ecliptic system. Changing from ecliptic to equatorial does not alter the distance of a body.

Declination is more familiar to astrologers than celestial latitude. Many astrologers quite routinely use declinations to establish the existence of *parallels* and *contraparallels,* which are treated as if they were a kind of aspect. Many astrologers have asserted that in using declinations they are using the vertical dimension of the horoscope, but this is not in fact quite true. The vertical dimension corresponding to the usually used horizontal dimension, celestial longitude, is celestial *latitude,* not declination. Declination comes from the *equatorial system,* as we have just shown. This is only the first of many problems in the astrological treatment of the vertical coordinates. For in most spherical coordinate systems the vertical coordinate is exactly at right angles to the reference plane. Declinations are not perpendicular to the ecliptic. But it should be realized that what has just been said about declinations has absolutely no bearing on the validity of parallels and contraparallels. It does, however, suggest that parallels and contraparallels of latitude should be investigated.

At this point we have covered the basic definitions that needed to be covered in order to understand the material that follows. Some additional technical concepts will be introduced further on, however, as the need arises.

The First Problem: Aspects

Now we are going to raise some of the concrete problems and questions posed by the existence of the latitude of planets. In most cases these are not very severe, but in some cases can be quite severe.

Here is a typical example, which is not uncommon. On 3 July 1939 the Moon conjoined Mars in longitude. At that time, the Moon had a latitude of +5N01 while Mars had latitude of −5S14. At the time of conjunction in *longitude*, the two bodies were therefore 10 degrees and 15 minutes apart in *latitude*. Thus two bodies ordinarily assumed to be in actual conjunction (by longitude measurement alone) were *not!* Was there or was there not a conjunction of the Moon and Mars on 3 July 1939? Was the conjunction affected at all by the latitude difference? If so, how?

Before the reader automatically assumes that latitude differences are not a factor, it should be recognized that there is at least one such aspect situation where it is generally agreed that latitude is a factor: the only difference between an ordinary lunation or new Moon and an eclipse of the Sun is that *in the eclipse the difference in latitude between the Sun and the Moon is very small* so that the bodies of the Sun and Moon *actually* do line up. In an ordinary lunation they do not. Why not take this into consideration with regard to conjunctions of other bodies? Many years ago Charles Jayne did considerable work on the subject of conjunctions between bodies that were at or near the same latitude. He called these conjunctions "line-ups" and found considerable evidence that *these were much more important than ordinary conjunctions.*

Another area where this is important is in relationships between natal and transiting planets. Is a transit by conjunction with a large latitude difference as powerful as one with a small latitude difference? One application of this idea suggested by Charles Jayne, both in an unpublished manuscript on line-ups and to me in personal conversations, is a means whereby long-range periods can be indicated by lunar transits to natal bodies. Lunar transits are usually considered to be too quick to make much of an impact except upon short-term emotional fluctuations. But Jayne's theory makes it possible for the Moon to indicate much longer emotional periods than mere transits of the normal type would indicate. Here is how it works.

The North and South Nodes of the Moon are the longitudes at which the transiting Moon has a latitude of zero. The latitude that the Moon may have at any degree, therefore, is determined by the distance in longitude between the nodes and the transiting Moon. The nearer the Moon is to a node, the nearer the latitude is to zero. Again an eclipse of the Sun is a Sun-Moon conjunction near the nodes.

Now let us say that Venus in the natal chart has a latitude of *x* degrees north, and that the Moon has that same latitude whenever it is *y* degrees beyond its North Node. This means that every time the transiting North Node of the Moon gets to the point where it is *y* degrees prior to the natal Venus (this is a rather slow transit), the transiting Moon will have the *same latitude as the natal Venus every time it conjoins Venus*. Now add to this the fact that the body of the Moon has a diameter of 30 minutes of arc, and it becomes clear that the transiting Moon will eclipse the position of the natal Venus for several months every time the two bodies are conjoined.

As we all know, eclipses appear to last for many months before and after. The conjunction in latitude as well as longitude could be an indication of a strong Moon-Venus period in the individual's life, which might not be visible by other means. This is a theory that is sufficiently plausible to be tried out. Simply watch to see if the transiting Moon is transiting natal planets *at the same latitude as the natal planets when it conjoins them*.

There are other latitude effects. Pluto can attain latitudes of up to plus or minus 17 degrees. At this writing it has a latitude of 17 N. This means that as Pluto transits any natal planets in Libra, it is likely to be out of orb of conjunction in terms of latitudinal criteria. Does this mean that Pluto is *not* going to affect these planetary energies? In some cases it seems so, in others not. It is not clear what the effect of Pluto's very high current latitude has on transits. But the question should not be ignored.

If you are interested in asteroids, then the problem gets much worse. Pallas' orbit is inclined to the Earth's at an angle of 31 degrees and 49 minutes. This means that Pallas can have extremely high latitudes. How will this affect the transits and conjunctions of Pallas?

Other aspects are affected as well by high latitude differences between pairs of bodies. Neither needs to have an extreme latitude as long as the difference between their latitudes is 10 degrees or more. All of the traditional aspects (oppositions, trines, square, sextiles, and so forth) *can be distorted by high latitude differences*. Should only positions on the ecliptic be considered important?

Fixed stars can have latitudes anywhere from 90 S to 90 N latitude. What is the longitude of a body at 90 N latitude? Answer: *all 360 degrees!* And the nearer a body gets to 90 N or 90 S the more indeterminate its longitude may get. Many astrologers glibly assert that the latitude of a fixed star makes no difference, even though *two bodies in ecliptic conjunction may be in square if latitude is considered!* If a fixed star at 18 Sagittarius is at 85 N latitude, it could be conjunct a planet at 18 Sagittarius with a latitude of 5 S, if only longitude is considered. However, in terms of the actual angular distance between them, the real distance is 90 degrees!! And when one considers other aspects, many fixed stars do not make sextiles and squares at all on the ecliptic, if latitude is taken into consideration.

My own opinion on this matter, and it is only an opinion, is that if two bodies are reasonably near the ecliptic, say plus or minus 20 degrees, the ecliptic angles between them may be significant, but that a high latitude difference between them *will alter the precise nature of the interaction*. How, I am not quite sure. I strongly urge astrologers to get into the study of this problem so that we can have some answers instead of opinions.

Latitude, Declination, Houses and Angles

Another extremely thorny area affected by latitude and declination involves the question of house position and angles. The following example will show how much the effect of latitude upon house position can be.

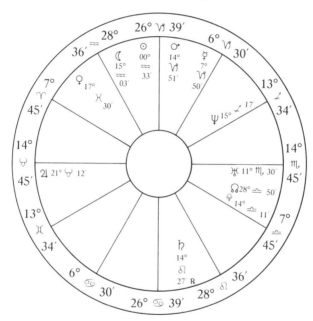

Jimmy Carter's Inauguration

President Jimmy Carter took the oath of office at 12:03 P.M., EST on 20 January 1977 in Washington, D.C. The chart for this is given in the conventional manner above. The house cusps used are according to the birthplace method of Koch, which is my personal preference for intermediate cusps. For those who prefer Placidus cusps and to demonstrate that this problem is not peculiar to Koch houses, here are the Placidus versions of the cusps. The MC and Ascendant being the same, only the intermediate cusps are given.

Eleventh House 22 Aqu 26   Second House 14 Tau 46
Twelfth House 28 Pis 07   Third House 13 Gem 02

According to either house system, in fact to almost any house system, Pluto is about 30 degrees down from the Descendant, well into the sixth house. However, if one calculates the Sidereal Time at which Pluto *actually* set, one gets a surprise. The sidereal time of the inauguration chart is 19:54:42. The sidereal time at which Pluto set in the latitude of Washington, D.C. was 19:52:23, only 00:02:19 of sidereal time earlier. In other words, Pluto was just barely below the west horizon at the time of the inauguration.

Uranus, you will note, is 27 degrees away from Pluto in longitude. However, Uranus set at 19:47:22 sidereal time, just four minutes prior to Pluto. They are very close in terms of their setting times. According to modern teachings, both planets are in the sixth house as the ecliptic chart shows, but they are *nowhere near as far into the sixth from the seventh as one might think*. If Carter had been inaugurated five minutes earlier, both Pluto and Uranus would still have appeared to be in the sixth house by longitude, but they would have been above the horizon! Most students of astrology would be willing to agree that a planet above the horizon cannot be in the sixth house. In the case of Uranus, the approximation shown by the conventional chart was not far off, but with Pluto, it would have been way off. Here are the latitudes of the planets at Carter's inauguration.

Sun	00 N 00
Moon	4 N 47
Mercury	2 N 25
Venus	0 S 09
Mars	0 S 48
Jupiter	0 S 53
Saturn	0 N 55
Uranus	0 N 27
Neptune	1 N 28
Pluto	17 N 09

Only Pluto has an extreme latitude, and only Pluto's house position could be questionable. Incidentally, while Pluto may in fact have set at the actual time of Carter's inauguration, we are not off the hook.

According to the Greeks and most authorities up until modern times, houses begin about five degrees prior to the cusps calculated in exactly this manner. Older authorities were well aware of this problem and took it into consideration. Considerable historical research has convinced me that it was not a change of opinion based on experience that caused later astrologers to stop paying attention to the latitude problem, *it was their inability to handle the mathematics involved.* Nineteenth-century astrologers were quite adept at spherical trigonometry and used it routinely in evaluating charts, but few later astrologers cared to take the touble. The astrology-made-simple movement took over and anything that couldn't be made simple was ignored. No wonder many astronomers have been contemptuous of astrology!

Times have changed, however, and with the rise of calculators and home computers, technical astrology has become easier to handle. Maybe now this problem will be handled with the attention that I feel it deserves. Stated very simply the problem is this: one cannot be certain from an ecliptic chart alone what house is occupied by a planet with considerable latitude (over 4 degrees N or S) when that planet is near a cusp. The only exception to this rule are those house systems in which the ecliptic longitude alone is the criterion for placing a planet in a house. Such systems would include Equal, Porphyry, and the so-called system of Morinus as popularized by Edward Lyndoe in *American Astrology* magazine.

Let's look at the diagram that will serve to make the source of the difficulty clearer. This particular diagram concerns the Ascendant, but what it shows applies to all other house cusps as well.

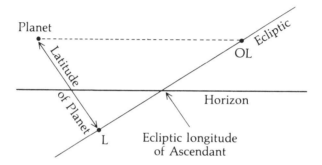

Diagram Concerning the Ascendant and Other House Cusps

In the diagram, the horizontal line is, appropriately enough, the horizon. The long line inclined to it represents the ecliptic. It should be recognized that all of the lines in this diagram are in fact arcs, but in order to make the diagram simpler, I have represented all arcs as straight lines. This does not affect the accuracy of the representation. Now note the dot that signifies the planetary body with latitude. The distance from the planet to the point on the ecliptic marked L is the latitude of the body. The point L itself represents the point of the body's longitude. The Ascendant is the point where the horizon intersects the ecliptic. The point OL is the point on the ecliptic that was on the horizon at the same time the planet was.

Here is the important part: the longitude, L, of the body is below the horizon in the first house, while the planetary body itself is above the horizon in what would be by most standards the twelfth house. What house is the planet truly in? I would say the twelfth house, but most astrologers looking at a conventional chart would have said the first house. It is not completely clear who is correct; however, the point is that most astrologers have not even examined the question.

As we have already pointed out, with fixed stars the problem becomes more acute. The following examples from my own horoscope will serve to make the point.

In my own horoscope, the right ascension of the Midheaven (simply the sidereal time expressed in degrees instead of hours) is 352 degrees and 14 minutes of arc. This gives an MC of 21 Pis 33 and an Ascendant, at 40 N 37, of 12 Can 22. The longitude of the star Sirius for 1942 is approximately 13 Can 17 with a latitude of 39 S 35. Many astrologers who used fixed stars have looked at my chart and stated that I have Sirius rising; how marvelous! However, there is one small problem. If one takes latitude into consideration, Sirius does not rise on the date of my birth until the right ascension of the Midheaven gets to 25 degrees and 29 minutes, about 2 hours and 13 minutes after my birth. That is a very large orb for a conjunction with the horizon! Similarly, the star Betelgeuse has a longitude of 27 Gem 38 and a latitude of 16 S 02. It does not appear to be anywhere near my birth horizon from a consideration of longitude alone. However, if we take latitude into consideration, we find that Betelgeuse rose at a right ascension of the Midheaven of 351 degrees and 19 minutes, which is quite close to my natal right ascension of the Midheaven. In these terms, I have Betelgeuse rising, not Sirius.

Positive Applications of Latitude and Declination Principles

Thus far we have talked mostly about problems that arise because of not considering latitude or declination. Mostly we have talked about latitude rather than declination, but it should be recognized that *not considering declination gives rise to essentially the same problems as not considering latitude*. Both are *vertical* dimensions in spherical coordinates, and not considering any vertical dimension in a coordinate system is likely to create problems. Let us now turn to ideas that *do* take the vertical dimension of the coordinate system into consideration. We shall find that some very powerful techniques arise when we do.

Parans

Although there are differences in the detail, both astrological tradition and research tell us that planets acquire greater impact on the chart when they are near an angle, i.e. the Ascendant, the Midheaven, the Descendant or Imum Coeli. Research by Gauquelin and others indicates that the peak of a planet's energy is in the middle to late cadent houses. Tradition suggests that it is near the angles in the angular houses. While this difference is important from certain points of view, it is not important to what follows.

Whatever the detailed truth may be, it is clear that planets have a fourfold rhythm of intensity. Each planet peaks in influence four times a day as it rises, culminates, sets and makes its lower culmination. Now let us suppose that two planets are situated such that they will *both transit angles simultaneously*, possibly the same angle as in simultaneous rising, or different angles, as with one rising while the other sets or culminates. It would seem logical to suppose that if this situation arises, the two planets' peaking cycles would be at least somewhat coordinated. Might this not link the energies of the two planets in a manner similar to an aspect? For example, if on a certain day Saturn rises with Mars culminating, then the Saturn rising peak will coincide with the Mars culminating peak, causing a Mars and Saturn peak of energy to coincide, thus linking Mars and Saturn.

This is not merely an hypothesis. Not only have many modern astrologers checked this out and found that it works, but it is in fact one of the most ancient of all astrological indications. The Babylonians used these angle linkings long before aspects on the ecliptic. One has to remember that Babylonian astrology was an observational one, and that the horizon and meridian circles (the circle going from north to south over one's head) are much more easily seen outdoors than the ecliptic. Ptolemy discusses these linkings in the *Almagest* at great length. Unfortunately, not too much has been stated about the influence of these linkings, but there are enough ancient records left to indicate that they were considered to be important. They were called in Greek "paranatellonta" in plural and "paranatellon" in singular. Modern astrologers have shortened the term to *parans* plural and *paran* singular. They appear to represent a direct and powerful linking of planetary energies, although it is not clear what differences there might be among the various types of parans.

The importance of parans for this discussion is that *they take latitude and declination into consideration*. The important thing is not that two bodies will conjoin two angles in longitude, but that together they cross the great circles (the horizon and meridian) that define the angles. It is important to note, incidentally, the following fact about parans. The two planets in question do not need to be actually on the angles in a chart to be in a paran. They only need to be in such a relationship that, if the earth were rotated until these planets came to the angles, *they would both cross the angles together*. It has also been demonstrated that paran relationships between natal and transiting bodies—in other words, paran transits—can be important.

Another fact about parans is that they depend upon the latitude of location. The important thing is not that two bodies will conjoin two angles in longitude, but that they cross the great circle of the horizon or meridian. Thus paran transits are affected by changing geographic latitude.

How to Find Parans

The mathematics of finding parans is a bit complicated, involving extensive spherical trig. However, some of the major computer services have added them to their list of options. In particular, Neil Michelsen's Astro Computing Services in San Diego, California, does these calculations. The usual format is to give the sidereal time or the right ascension of the Midheaven at the time each of the bodies would rise, culminate, set and make the lower culmination. Thus there are four S.T.'s or RAMC's per planet. *If any one of the four S.T.'s or RAMC's of any planet is conjunct any one of the four S.T.'s or RAMC's of another planet, they are in paran.* Here is an example.

	RAMC (R)	RAMC (M)
Sun	229 52	302 45
Moon	235 44	316 05
Mercury	206 13	278 22
Venus	262 41	348 34
Mars	216 39	286 13
Jupiter	304 33	49 01
Saturn	32 34	137 12
Uranus	141 34	219 12
Neptune	182 25	254 12
Pluto	101 22	199 44

	RAMC (S)	RAMC (I)
Sun	15 38	122 45
Moon	36 25	136 05
Mercury	350 32	98 22
Venus	74 28	168 34
Mars	355 46	106 13
Jupiter	153 29	229 01
Saturn	251 50	317 12
Uranus	296 51	39 12
Neptune	325 59	74 12
Pluto	298 06	19 44

In Carter's inauguration chart, Pluto has a setting RAMC of 298 degrees and 6 minutes. Uranus has a setting RAMC of 296 degrees and 51 minutes. There is a *setting paran* between Uranus and Pluto that is made even more potent by the fact, pointed out earlier in this article, that they are also both on the west horizon at the time. This is an angular paran. Not all parans are angular.

Another example in Carter's inaugural chart is the Sun with a rising RAMC of 229 degrees and 52 minutes, while Jupiter has a lower culmination RAMC of 229 degrees and 1 minute. Here we have a Sun rising, Jupiter lower-culminating paran even though the Sun is not setting and Jupiter is not making its lower culmination. In fact the Sun is just about to make its upper culmination, and is within 4 degrees (about the orb I would recommend) of making the Sun upper-culmination, Uranus and Pluto setting paran. As the Sun progresses in this chart, about two years after his inauguration the Sun makes an *upper culmination, Jupiter a rising paran.* On this basis, I predicted at the time of the inauguration that Carter's first two years in office would not amount to much, largely because of strong opposition to his administration from various other power groups, mostly Congress. In about two years, however, he would begin to take control and would become a more effective president. This appears to be happening as of this writing (January 1979). At any rate, this is an example of the practical use of parans in astrology.

Declination, Parallels and Parans

What is a parallel? We know what it is mathematically, of course, but we are not too clear about why it has significance. It has already been pointed out that declination is not the vertical dimension of longitude. *It is the vertical dimension of right ascension.* So why do parallels have significance? The answer, I believe, is connected with parans.

Because of the geometry of planetary transits over the angles, one cannot say that if Saturn rises while Mars culminates, Saturn will necessarily culminate while Mars sets. In other words, a paran on one pair of angles does not mean that there will be parans on other pairs of angles at the same time. There is an exception to this, however. *If two bodies are also in parallel of declination when they are in paran,* they will *always* transit the angles in pairs and be in paran on any pair of angles. Contraparallels also synchronize the rising, culminating, setting and lower culmination patterns of pairs of planets, but not as perfectly as parallels. I suspect, therefore, that parallels of declination are of the same family of linkage that parans are and are not related to zodiacal aspects at all. Otherwise there is no reasonable explanation for parallels and contra-parallels that I can conceive of. Note that eclipses of the Sun are also parallels and that the Sun conjunct Moon while parallel Moon will transit all angles simultaneously. Thus an eclipse is both a zodiacal aspect and a paran aspect. Maybe this is part of the reason eclipses are so powerful.

Conclusions

As I indicated earlier, this article has raised more questions than it has answered, but if this causes more astrologers to look at things that they have taken for granted in astrology, then I will have accomplished my purpose. It is quite clear to me that the problems and opportunities for new methods indicated by the latitude and declination questions can have important consequences for practicing astrologers. But this will only be true if astrologers will examine the issues instead of taking refuge in the old line "but my way of doing it works. Why should I look at another way?" Until we know *why* our ways of doing things apparently work, we are not justified in being complacent.

10

Symbols of the Father Complex

I would like to define some things so that we don't have a complete misunderstanding of what it is that we are talking about. When I say the "father complex," I am not talking about an exaggerated set of patterns in a personality, such as a complex about this or that. Complex simply means a group of interacting symbols. I am talking about father symbolism and not a pathological manifestation of father symbolism. That is the first point. The second point is, what do I mean by father? I don't mean the male progenitor. There are basically two archetypal styles of parenting, which are loosely associated with the parents of the same name, but every mother is to some extent a father figure, and every father is to some extent a mother figure. In some cases the roles are completely reversed and in most cases they vary in mixtures. So we are talking about the archetypal role of parenting, not the masculine parent.

The two types of parenting, mothering and fathering, can be symbolically related to the 4-10 axis. The fourth house is the symbol of nurture, support, where you have come from, your roots, your origins; the tenth is your external social role, where you are headed in society. The mother figure is the person who provides the unconditional nurture and support that is needed to sustain you physically and emotionally in the physical universe. The father figure is that set of persons or institutions, particularly the last, that guides you in taking on a role in society. I think the major difference between these two figures, aside from the different thrust of direction, is that love and nurture are provided unconditionally in the mother complex; whereas in the father complex they are provided conditionally. You have to achieve and perform to a certain set of standards. Who you are is not as significant as what you do. In the mother complex, who you are is much more fundamental. Obviously the father complex, when it is exaggerated, can have some pathological effects; but basically the father figure is a person who initiates you into the rules of the game, so that you can play it. Without the father complex operating, you are in no position to play the game at any level whatsoever.

There is no one symbol or planet in astrology that correlates to the father complex. That is one of the reasons I use the term "complex." It is a mixture of symbols operating interactively and some of the symbols have roles not directly related to the father complex.

What are the components of the father complex? Traditionally the father complex is said to be symbolized by the Sun and Saturn. While incomplete, this is not wrong. The Sun and Saturn signify the father figure in two different roles. The Sun is basically two different things. First of all, it is a source of energy by which one is maintained. The Sun as the symbol of the father figure symbolizes that aspect of the father figure that supplies the energy for the whole system to maintain itself; that is, the father is the breadwinner. Many of these aspects do not necessarily correlate with the biological father. As a matter of fact the public school system is more often what people encounter as the father archetype because the parent is usually off trying to make a living, and is seldom around to make a strong impact. Every time a mother disciplines the child she is acting as the father. Any time she says: "There, there, dear, I'll love you no matter what," she is acting as the mother archetype.

The Sun not only symbolizes the father as energy source but also as role model. As a person develops, the Sun ceases to be part of the father complex and becomes a part of the fundamental identity of the individual. So there is a transition of the Sun from out there as another person who acts as a role model and as an energy source. Gradually, the Sun is introjected into the self to become one's fundamental self-expressive energy. There is a very powerful linkup between the Sun as father archetype and the Sun as me being me: "Here I am, world, and this is what I can do." The Sun at some point changes courses in this way.

Saturn, on the other hand, is that aspect of the father that is the initiator into the rules of the game. Actually I have to pair up Saturn and Jupiter because Jupiter is also part of the father archetype. Without one you can't understand the other in this function.

The ideal father does two things. He says to the child: "Here is what you must do to become an acceptable member of society. I will assist you in doing it, and by the time you are ready to face the tests and trials to prove you have done it, you will be ready. I will support you all the way through." The demand is made but the support system is provided to insure that the child will be ready to reach that level. This is the more Jupiterian aspect of the father. Then there is the more savage aspect of the father, essentially proceeding from a position of: "When you assume a role in society you will replace me. In order to insure that you will replace me only when you are worthy, I am going to resist you as much as possible." This sounds totally negative, but it isn't. Only when people encounter that kind of resistance can they really affirm to themselves that they have room. This is the Saturnian aspect of the father. It is that aspect of the father which is symbolized in primitive initiation rituals where the men of the tribe come to the twelve-year-old boy in terrifying costumes, threatening to castrate him; even forcing the child into a death-and-rebirth ritual. Generally speaking, the child does not feel terrifically supported by this aspect of the father figure. This is the aspect of the father figure that is symbolized by Saturn eating his own children.

Jupiter basically teaches social integration and is a synthesizing energy. How do you become a functioning part of a whole? How do you relate to the whole and in what ways will you embody the ethos of the whole? There are really two aspects to the planet Jupiter: One pertains to the father complex, and the other does not. There is the Jupiter that simply wants to get as much experience as possible, to be free, with as little structure as possible. That is the non-father aspect of Jupiter. The other aspect of Jupiter is that which is totally involved with the idea of social integration, of making the individual a part of the whole, of understanding the frameworks that bind the whole together—religion, philosophy. This is the paternal aspect of Jupiter.

(My credentials are Saturn opposing the Sun and in 45-degree aspect to Jupiter, which is rising in the first house and in a grand trine with Mars and the Midheaven. I feel I come before you with a classic Jupiter-Saturn mix.)

The Jupiter usually starts out first as the non-father aspect. When the individual discovers that there are limits, restraints, restrictions, this is when he encounters the Saturn. Then Jupiter metamorphoses as a symbol into the second aspect.

There are also two kinds of Sagittarians. Type-one Sagittarius is the one you read about most frequently—very effervescent, jolly, friendly, freedom-oriented, one who loves the outdoors and is almost impossible to tie down. Then there is the more serious one who is basically involved in the investigation of everything. Type-two Sagittarius is related to the father aspect of Jupiter.

Now ideally these two aspects of Jupiter and Saturn must be balanced in the developing personality. If you have a situation where the support of a father is considerably less stressed than the resistance by the father, then you have a child who has a serious Saturn problem. These I have seen in horoscopes where Saturn is conjunct an angle, aspecting the Sun—most outstandingly by hard aspect, but you can see this with a soft aspect sometimes, too, if other things support it. Saturn aspecting Mars, particularly by hard aspect, plus a general deficiency of Jupiter would indicate this type of personality. Those are the signs of the negative father complex.

The end result of the father complex, which is why it is so terribly important to understand, is that it creates within the individual the archetype of reality. It is my philosophical position that there is possibly an infinite number of realities, and we just happened to have arbitrarily chosen to play our game in a particular one. In order to play the game of reality, we have to become convinced that it is real! At some point we can transcend this and recognize that it is an interesting construct and not absolutely determined, but initially we have to get sucked into the game to take it seriously. Among the people who don't get sucked into the game are people with extremely active Neptunes. You find that on the one hand, they are very spiritual and on the other hand, extremely unreliable. They are not dishonest in the ordinary sense of the word. They are not putting falsehood in place of the truth. They are generally unaware of the distinction. You can't really fault them when they lie to you, because they generally believe that what they are saying is true. They happen to create a reality system that your reality system does not share. Then there are those who consciously lie, which is another whole issue. The creation of a reality system is probably the most important aspect of a father complex. It is to these aspects that one looks to see what kind of reality a person has. Along with that, I might add the things going on with the ninth house, which also has to do with the reality system, especially as it relates to one's belief system.

A heavily Saturnine view of reality is one which can best be exemplified by the conventional scientific idea of reality, that being the current most powerful representative of the Saturn school of thought. The only path toward truth, it holds, is the path of pure objectivism in which we try to transcend our individual points of view and get a God's-eye perspective on the whole thing. There is nothing wrong with this, because insofar as we have a consensus reality, this is an extremely useful way of getting in touch with it; but, this view does, as we all know, have pathological aspects. If someone sees things differently than you do, you are forced to prove that person wrong, or you are forced to acknowledge yourself wrong. In the first case, one person is maimed, and in the other case, the other person is maimed; nobody comes out ahead. If you have a more cosmopolitan or cosmic viewpoint, you may be willing to acknowledge that in that person's space, it is a valid reality, but not in yours, which is perfectly OK. That is not a Saturnine view of reality.

Another aspect of Saturnine reality is the idea of significance. Most people feel that what they do has to have a point, that is, life is not simply lived for its own sake, but rather there is some cosmic purpose being served. It may be anything from "I am going to become the Chairman of GM," to "I am going to be the prophet of the one God." Most of us experience severe states of anxiety when we encounter the possibility that we are utterly insignificant. Most of our systems of reality are quite Saturnine. I would even say, pathologically Saturnine. This is an extemely Saturnine culture when it comes to reality. I myself am torn, on the one hand, believing in the essentially arbitrary nature of reality, and on the other, trying to do statistical studies of astrological phenomena to find out what is really true! All you are doing in that kind of study is trying to get a firmer grip on the consensus reality. Someone with enough magical power might seriously distort the whole thing and make it work out quite differently.

Saturn, particularly as the most dominant characteristic of the father complex, is incapable of getting in touch with the idea that a thing may be an end unto itself. There is a serious problem with this. Let us suppose that we have an activity that serves a higher purpose. That makes us more significant. The next time you start talking about giving your soul to God or doing some similar thing, you may be doing it because it covertly makes you feel more significant. Let's suppose your activity serves a higher purpose. As you look at it consciously, you are forced to ask, "Then what purpose does that purpose serve?", and now you have to find an even higher purpose. Eventually you have to find a still higher purpose, because if at any time the purposes being served themselves serve no other purpose, then everything beneath serves no purpose either. Eventually you get to a point where the chain of justification stops, and you are forced to deal with an activity that is pursued entirely for its own sake. Such an activity is a game, because a game is pursued entirely for its own sake. A game is not necessarily trivial, however, which is something we should get clear about. Finally, if one believes in a conventional notion of Deity, one arrives at Deity and one comes to the conclusion that all these higher works are doing nothing but serving the Deity's game. What is the Deity doing? Why is the Deity doing it? You have to postulate a Deity's Deity or quit. I choose to quit. What you wind up with, then, is the notion that the highest purpose is no purpose at all. The purpose was without purpose. What you have to get in touch with is that being insignificant is not significant. Its significance is also not significant. You wind up with the idea that all that is really going on here is a beautiful, gigantic, wonderful and sometimes rather ghastly (depending on which chapter of the book you happen to be in) cosmic game. It is simply the universe doing its own thing, and we all happen to be part of the thing it is doing. We could not fail to serve its purposes even if we tried, because we are part of it. When a person first makes this discovery, which is actually a form of enlightenment, we call it alienation. Alienation is a Saturn disease, because the person has come to half the truth, which is, "Yes, it is true that I am pointless, that my life has no purpose, except the one I choose to give it, but even that is purposeless." What most people don't get is the second truth, which is, "It's OK that my life is pointless. So my life becomes a pure unfolding of my internal energies like a flower." At that point we are liberated from all kinds of incredible weight that the father complex has placed on all of us. At the same time, we had to experience the father complex to get to a real understanding of what is going on. This has been rather abstract so far, so let me give you something concrete.

Before continuing, I want to say that the tenth house is also part of the father complex. There has been a raging controversy in astrology for these last

2,000 years as to which house is which parent. I think my answer is fairly clear, but again, I have to stress that the tenth house does not necessarily, or even usually, signify one's biological father. Neither the fourth nor the tenth signify either parent consistently. What I do is look to see which parent fulfills the symbolism of which house better, and then I make the identification. If you have a Gemini father and Mercury in your tenth house, the tenth house is probably your father. Sometimes you get a terrifically heavy Moon in the tenth, then you know it is very motherly. Exaggerated father complexes produce a number of psychological characteristics, and I think we can start by saying that the extreme ones are, in psychological terminology, obsessive-compulsive types—the ones who are extremely cleanliness-oriented, very concerned with every detail being exactly right—people who have a vise on their emotions. These are all typical examples of an excessive father complex in the horoscope. The ones that are the most striking are the Mars-Saturn-Sun afflictions, which are even more potent if the tenth house is involved. In this case the word "affliction" is appropriate, because it is experienced as an afflicting set of circumstances.

There is a man who has a Mars-Saturn conjunction in the tenth house, which is exact within 5 minutes of arc squaring the Sun in the seventh within 2 degrees of arc. Both the Sun-Saturn and Mars are potential indications of an over-developed father complex, and the Mars-Saturn in the tenth reinforces the theme. This is a blatant astrological case of an over-developed father complex. Now for the person behind it. He is very sensitive and feeling, yet self-compelled to suppress all of that in a very powerful drive for success and achievement. But he has not succeeded. The result is that he has a terrible self-image and takes refuge in alcohol. His Moon is in the twelfth house, bisecting the angle between his Mars-Saturn conjunction and Neptune. He went to college and assumed immediately and correctly that his family expected him to be a lawyer, doctor, architect, physicist or something like that, regardless of his own inclination. This total suppression of individual identity in favor of what I will call "everybody else's ego" is characteristic of an over-developed father complex. In addition, his father is the finest example of a Jungian terrible father I have ever personally known. By terrible father, I am not referring to a father who neglects and does not pay any attention to his children. I am referring to the position that: "My sons one day are going to displace me, unless I now, while they are young, permanently emasculate them." The classic Saturn-Cronos-eating-his-children trip. This man systematically tried to convince all of his sons (who are all brilliant) that they are stupid, incompetent, incapable of holding their own in the real world. The oldest son got the brunt of it and he is one of the brightest people I have ever known. A funny thing has happened. You can tell he is the most sucked in, because he is the only person who respects his father. None of the other sons do. In addition to admiring his father, he finally wound up going into the same business as his father, which is characteristic of an over-developed father complex, with males particularly.

I have a Sun-Saturn opposition, and it was my father who got me into astrology. I have followed in my father's footsteps also, except that in my case it happened to be appropriate. In my friend's case it was not particularly appropriate. No matter how successful he is at being a general contractor, unless he goes through some sort of therapy or enlightenment experience, he is never going to be happy with what he has done. He is only going to be aware of how he has failed. This is a characteristic of an over-developed father pattern, particularly when Saturn is the dominant energy in it. In other words, his father has essentially succeeded in his original objective of keeping him down. My friend designed his own house with no architectural training whatsoever. The workmanship is magnificent, interesting and functionally useful. His father came in and pointed out all the flaws. This is a typical kind of pattern.

Just to show you how this can be modified, there is another person who was born a couple of years later who has the Mars-Saturn conjunction squaring the Sun in the eleventh house instead of the tenth, with the Sun in the eighth. She has Venus and Neptune in the tenth. Her father is one of those really elegant, wise old gentlemen who has a high standard of excellence. She idealized him (Venus and Neptune in Libra in the tenth). She is totally unaware of the fact that without any coercion, any conscious force on his part, she has been sold a bill of goods; that unless she is absolutely number one in her field, she is no one. She is a musician. Just to prove to you that an over-developed father complex is not all that bad, her first job was playing in a major symphony orchestra. She has played in major orchestras ever since. Now, your ordinary, average person would consider that an achievement, but her objective is to become the greatest living player of her instrument. Unfortunately, she does not quite have it. Because she is so tense, she does not allow the soul to come through. That is also a characteristic of an over-developed father complex. The energy that is propelling her to success is also inhibiting it. The part that is really grim, from the standpoint of her happiness, is that if she ever did overcome this tension and become the greatest performer on her instrument, she would then have to become the greatest musician, and if she succeeded in that, she would have to go on to some other game, constantly upping the stakes. This is the behavioral syndrome of the over-developed father complex. Success from the subjective point of view is essentially impossible.

On the other hand, persons with this sort of psychological complex are people who as a rule can be very sucessful. They are either total failures or very successful—that is, other people acknowledge them as successful. The classic over-developed father type does not know how to handle praise and will acknowledge any criticism with a thousand times more intensity than any amount of praise. So you get cautiousness and conservatism, barring of course, a strong Uranus. In its extreme form, you get reactionaries. A reactionary is basically a person who is protecting his reality trip. When you have this kind of intense investment in reality, anything that is inconsistent with your reality is viewed literally as a death threat.

Reality structures are a very important part of the father complex. Very closely related to this are "ego structures." Ego is also a direct encounter with the father complex. The ego can be understood as the psychological counterpart of the physical body. As the body is the physical interface between the soul and the universe, the ego is the psychological interface between the soul and the universe. It is that set of structures by which we set up our relationship to the universe in which we live. It consists basically of three parts:

Part one makes each of us feel that we have a unique orientation in time-space: "My experience and actions are not your experience and actions." I associate this unique orientation with the meridian axis in the horoscope. Not just the top or the bottom, but both ends together. When you bring in the whole thing, you realize that it must have a connection with the father complex, because the upper meridian has a connection with the father complex.

The second component of the ego complex is: "Not only is my action and experience me—but I am also not you." This sense of separateness to some extent is symbolized in the horoscope by the horizon (me vs. them—the Ascendant vs. the seventh house). Even more, it is symbolized by the actions of the planet Saturn. Saturn is the single factor that is most responsible for creating the appearance of separateness. Separation is one of the valid keywords for Saturn. Here again, that is part of the father complex.

The third component of the ego complex is basically that part of you which says: "This is what I am, I am going to be what I am, and no matter how much pressure there is for me to be something else, I will be what I am." This, the will-to-be, is both the Sun and Mars. The Sun again is part of the father complex.

The Sun as father, being the role model, is the individual who gives us the idea that we are someone in particular. Saturn as father gives us the idea that I am not you; and the father is once again a role model and definer of social obligations and relationships. The Midheaven also has to do with creating our unique sense of orientation in time and space.

Basically, an over-developed father complex in the horoscope can be analyzed as an over-developed ego. Immediately one tends to think that this means too aggressive or dominant, but that is only one type of over-developed ego. The sense that you are totally alone, isolated and separate from other people is also over-developed ego. The sense that your experience has no relation to other people's experience is also an over-developed ego. Just as there are three components to the ego complex, there are three kinds of over-developed ego.

An over-developed father complex tends to amplify those parts of the ego that have to do with separateness and with having a unique orientation in time-space. Oddly enough, these two characteristics diminish the will-to-be, because they set up a dialectic between your Sun, which is at this point internalized, and Saturn, the demands and role expectations of other people. For example, after the words, "mommy" and "daddy," what are the first words that most kids use? The answer is, "no" and "me."

What the "no" symbolism conflicts with is "Yes you will, damn it!" What you come up against is the non-personal will, other people's will, demands and role expectations. You go into a dialectic; the two of them push against each other—what the parent wants, what the child wants. These go back and forth until a balance is achieved and you have a mature, adult ego, in the sense of the will-to-be. If the father complex is over-developed, then the child's own sense of will-to-be is thwarted. In this case you get a person who is primarily interested in living up to other people's expectations. He or she may be very good at it, like a person who has to achieve what other people define as success.

When I am not watching what I am doing I get sucked into other people's role expectations. It is only when I am conscious that I fight. This is the kind of "heroic" activity in which we all get involved. We are all heros in some area, and this is our Sun, which started out as our internalized father figure and is now trying to express itself. So the people who have an over-developed Saturn have to overcome Saturn, which defines you according to what everyone else says. Or, as R.D. Laing put it, "The everyone which is everywhere elsewhere." What the neighbors will think is a manifestation of Saturn.

The over-developed father complex tends to create an adult ego form which is very high on alienation (a sense of uniqueness and aloneness) and very low on a will-to-be (what it would determine itself to be if it had the freedom). This is in contrast to the Neptunian self-sacrificer who does not have a will-to-be. The over-developed Saturn type has a very strong will-to-be, but it happens to be relatively squashed. The Neptunian self-sacrificer never had a will-to-be in the first place, which is why it was so easy to give it up.

There is a question about a stressful aspect involving Neptune, Saturn and the Sun. Here you would have a condition where the person has no strong will-to-be yet at the same time has a very strong sense that there are external obligations and duties. The will-to-be in this case is sufficiently weakened so that the person can't live up to these obligations, even if the person chooses to. This is almost a guaranteed failure program. It does not mean that the person will be a failure in every area of his or her life. There will usually be some area in which he or she will say "I failed here," and "I am no good, because I have failed here." What the person has to do is immediately get to the position where he or she doesn't have to be anything in order to be OK. At the same time, the person has to give whatever he or she has to something that is so far beyond him or her that the persons's own strength and ability is no longer a question. The support comes from some transcendental idea or cause. I would find the person some ascetic, spiritual discipline or cause. In its positive manifestation, Saturn-Neptune is the symbol of the monk who lives in a simple, bare cell with nothing by way of physical pleasure, pursuing a relentless spiritual discipline. This is often an acceptable path for these people although when you introduce it to a lot of them, even if it is appropriate for them, their immediate reaction is far from happy. I don't mean literally being a monk, but they have to surrender their lives to a higher Power. A lot of people who have this kind of condition are becoming fundamentalists, which is not a path I would particularly recommend, but if it works, why not. That is a Saturn-Neptune-Mars-Sun kind of path. Saturn-Neptune is also the symbol of the depressive in its negative manifestation.

There is a question as to the power of the planets in angular and cadent houses. I basically buy the research results of the Gauquelins. The only question I have about their research is that it was done largely on famous individuals. There is no question that the planets are strong in the ninth and twelfth houses, but my impression of twelfth-house energies is that people usually can't handle them. It seems to me that the difference between the really successful professionals and the more ordinary people is the degree to which they are able to handle the very intense energies of the twelfth-house planets. For example, I have Saturn in the Gauquelin plus zone for scientists and Jupiter in the Gauquelin minus zone for scientists. This suggests that I may be intrinsically a scientist, but that I lack the discipline to work in that manner.

To be important, generational aspects like Saturn-Neptune must tie into something personal in the horoscope, aspecting the Sun or Moon or the angles, or perhaps, less potently, Mercury, Venus or Mars. Otherwise, people will not express the Saturn-Neptune traits. Almost everybody born in 1953 has a Saturn-Neptune conjunction in Libra, but not all, by any means, are classic Saturn-Neptune types. In fact most of them that I have met are not; but the ones who are, oh boy! Particularly the conjunction squaring Uranus. The negative side of it contributes to anxiety and fanaticism.

There is a question as to a square to Saturn with a trine to it. Trines do not necessarily represent a mitigation. It depends on what the planetary symbols are themselves. I have seen serious father complexes symbolized by a mass of trines involving the Sun, Mars and Saturn. The squares tend to manifest as critical episodes and to be clearly delineated as happening at certain points and times. The trine is an on-going pattern that is so normal, regularized, and stable that you don't even notice it is there, but that doesn't make it any easier. Crises are actually easier to deal with because it is something you can put your finger on. With trines you can't put your finger on anything, so people think they are OK. If you are into the "no news is good news" school of life, then a trine is OK because it doesn't represent news, but a steady, on-going set of circumstances. This was put very well by a Cleveland doctor who said that in his work with illnesses he found that squares and hard aspects indicate acute episodes and trines and sextiles indicate chronic diseases.

There is a question as to how you would fit Pluto into the father complex. It is not intrinsically a part of the father complex. When Pluto is tied to the symbols of the father complex it gives the paternal energy a much more ruthless and maniacal kind of aspect—much more fanatical. The power struggle that ensues is very intense, and the idea of actually destroying the child comes out with Pluto. Pluto can also mean an extremely intense involvement, which does not always work out that negatively. The real obsessive-compulsive is a Saturn-Pluto type: the "I have to get my hands clean" sort of thing. Pluto is not intrinsically related to the father or mother complex. Pluto can come into either one.

There is a question as to your being apt to carry on with *your* child your exaggerated father or mother complex? The answer is "yes."

Fortunately, I have a daughter. She has no signs of an exaggerated father complex. She has the Sun exactly opposite Uranus and trine Neptune. She has Saturn operating, but it is in opposition to the Moon conjunct Jupiter; so she has symbols of a possible exaggerated mother complex. So far, everything seems to be working out OK. Apparently the sins that were visited upon me (not by my parents, but by the world in general) are not being visited upon her.

There is a question as to unaspected planets. At this point I tend to agree with the idea that Geoffrey Dean has put forth in his book *Recent Advances in Natal Astrology*, that they tend to operate in an unintegrated way. They either operate to the exclusion of everything else, or do not operate at all. They often oscillate back and forth. I believe that would be the case with an unaspected Saturn. I would expect a person normally lacking in discipline, but who is occasionally subject to tremendous bursts of highly disciplined activity during which everything else is cut out. That would be my guess.

Janice Joplin had an unaspected Mars and one of her biographers commented on how she alternated between periods of incredible lethargy and maniacal activity. I have an unaspected Moon and I am either emotionally detached or utterly overwhelmed. Dean has a definition of what he means by unaspected. He is not denying the validity of midpoints and minor aspects when he says this, but by "unaspected" he means not in any classical, Ptolemaic aspect (conjunction, sextile, square, trine or opposition) within a 5-degree orb. Aspects to the Nodes, Ascendant, Midheaven, Arabic parts and all non-planetary bodies do not count; neither do any semisextiles or quincunxes. The asteroids probably would count. That is not to say that a semisquare to an otherwise unaspected planet would not have a visible effect. The planet is not weak, it is just highly unintegrated. Neither would an angular planet be weak. Dean looks for groupings of planets where none of the planets in Group A have major aspects to group B, and he identifies these as being separate complexes within the personality.

The indication of an exaggerated mother complex is found in connection with the Moon, Venus and the fourth, which is the major house for this complex. An over-dominant mother complex tends to be found in persons who are abnormally dependent, have a very unformed idea of reality and are extremely subjective. An over-developed mother complex is just as bad as an over-developed father complex, but each of them can be handled. When you have indications of problems in both, one of them will tend to be over-developed and the other one, radically under-developed. The man with the Jungian terrible father is a classical case in point. The Moon in the twelfth at the midpoint of Mars-Neptune and Saturn-Neptune is an indication of an under-developed mother complex. His mother is a very bright woman who tends to be an alcoholic and who generally has not been able to withstand the influence of her husband.

There is a question as to the Sun-Moon conjunction—are the parents similar? They are not necessarily similar, but they are experienced as having complementary and harmonious influences, assuming that the conjunction is not in a discordant setup. What do you do when one brother has Sun square Moon and the other has Sun trine Moon? Their experience of the parents, not the parents themselves, is harmonious or discordant.

11

Dodekatemoria: An Ancient Technique Reexamined

In the writings of many of the ancient Greek authors on astrology one finds reference to a peculiar type of position referred to as the *dodekatemorion* or twelfth part. It is mentioned by Ptolemy, Julius Firmicus Maternus and Manilius, and is found repeatedly in the horoscopes published in Neugebauer's *Greek Horoscopes*. What is peculiar about these positions is that they are derived from the longitudes of the planets. They are then entered into the horoscope as auxiliary positions of the planets in much the same manner that many modern astrologers use the solstice points (or antiscia, as they are more correctly called). Thus, in effect, the number of positions in the chart is doubled. Aspects, house and sign placements are then taken as if they were simple planets. But we are getting ahead of ourselves.

The fact is that there were several methods of computing *dodekatemoria* and they were used in various ways. One of these methods has come down to us from Indian astrology as *dwadasamsas*, to use the Hindu term, but the other two have completely died out. Of these last two, one has been investigated both by me and other workers and has shown astonishing results. However, let us begin by looking at the three basic kinds of dodekatemoria.

Type One

The first type is the kind that has come to us as the dwadasamsa. It is simply one-twelfth of a sign, or two and one-half degrees. It is used or referred to by Ptolemy, Manilius and Julius Firmicus Maternus. Each sign is divided into twelve equal divisions, the first of which is allocated to the sign in which it is contained. The second division is for the next sign and so forth until the last division of the sign is reached. That division is given to the sign that is twelve signs away. This results in a discontinuous series of divisions. For example, the divisions of Aries would proceed from the first division, given to Aries, to the last division, given to Pisces. However, in Taurus the first division would be given to Taurus. Since the last division in Aries is given to Pisces, an Aries division is being skipped over. For this reason this first type of dodekatemoria does not qualify as a twelfth harmonic. Any true harmonic presents an unbroken series of signs from Aries through Pisces repeating for as many times as the number of the harmonic. Therefore, a true fifth harmonic would present a series of signs from Aries to Pisces five times in the 360 degrees of the zodiac.

In Hindu astrology the primary concern with the dwadasamsa is the sign in which it falls. Very seldom does one find a dwadasamsa horoscope with individual planetary degrees and house positions, and even when this is done, it is done as a chart unto itself. On the other hand, with the Greeks the dodekatemoria were placed in the conventional chart along with the normal positions. Some Greek authors who used this method of computing also regarded only the sign placements without reference to the individual degrees, but this does not seem to have been the general practice.

From the harmonic point of view the dwadasamsa type of dodekatemoria seems to be illogical, skipping a sign every twelve signs as it does. However, from the Greek point of view, which was concerned with logical and aesthetic elegance, it does have a certain simplicity. Of course each sign should start with its own dwadasamsa. Is the first degree of a sign not the most characteristic? Modern opinion might debate that, but it is not completely unreasonable.

The adoption of the dwadasamsa type of dodekatemoria has had some important consequences for Hindu astrology and also for modern Western astrology, which has been influenced by Hindu astrology. The direct use of dwadasamsas is the obvious instance, but there are others, which will be referred to below. For the remainder of this article, this type-one dodekatemoria will be referred to as dwadasamsas so as to prevent confusion.

Type Two

The second type of dodekatemoria could be described as lunar dodekatemoria. I am aware of only one source for this type and that is Manilius, who mentions it directly after discussing the dwadasamsa type. He makes it clear, however, that it is not his invention. The procedure here is to take the longitude of the Moon, and calculate its twelfth harmonic, i.e. its true twelfth harmonic, not the dwadasamsa. The sign of the lunar twelfth harmonic then becomes the sign of its dodekatemorion (singular form of the word). Then all dodekatemoria are counted from the Moon's. No examples of this technique are given and we have no idea how it was used. Therefore, let us go directly on to the next and last (as far as we know) type of dodekatemoria.

Type Three

As with the Greek usage of the dwadasamsa, this type also involved the computation of the actual degree and minute of the dodekatemorion of each planet. However, the computation varies. Here is Otto Neugebauer's description of the method of computation (O. Neugebauer and H.B. Van Hoesen, *Greek Horoscopes*, Philadelphia: American Philosophical Society, 1959, p.6):

> Assume a point A of a zodiacal sign being x degrees from the beginning of the sign. With A there is then associated as "dodekatemorion" another point B whose distance from A is 12x (and therefore from the beginning of the original sign 13x). This relationship is one of the rare instances where a similar doctrine is also known from cuneiform sources.

What we have here is dodekatemorion = x + 12x = 13x. In other words this dodekatemorion is a thirteenth harmonic, not a twelfth. Using the harmonic method of computing a harmonic position, we find that multiplying the longitudes by 13 and casting out the complete circles of 360 degrees gives us the same results as using Neugebauer's table.

These dodekatemoria are found in the horoscopes of Vettius Valens, quoted in Neugebauer. Vettius Valens was roughly a contemporary of Ptolemy and came after Manilius. Thus it might seem that this is a later type of dodekatemorion than the dwadasamsa. However, Neugebauer's indication that this type is found in cuneiform sources strongly suggests that it is older than the other two. And I believe that there is internal evidence to suggest that the dwadasamsa is a corrupted form of it.

First of all, in Hindu astrology, which appears to spring from the same sources as Greek astrology and was also strongly influenced by it, there are a number of zodiacal subdivisions. Most of these are true harmonics in the sense that there are a number of repeated zodiacal sequences as one proceeds around the zodiac. However, the three most obvious deviations from this principle are the one-third divisions, or decanates, the one-quarter divisions, known in India as *chatturthamsas*, and the dwadasamsas. Most of the others have true harmonic bases. It appears as if there was at one time a highly evolved and harmonically oriented system of astrology in the Middle Eastern part of the world extending as far east as India. If there was such a system, it appears to have become corrupted fairly extensively so that only fragments survive in Western astrology. More has survived in India but much of the lore has been forgotten or misunderstood. The implication of this is that the non-harmonic subdivisions in Hindu astrology might be corruptions of harmonic ones.

Also there was a very important change from Babylonian to Greek astrology, a change in emphasis from time as cycles to time as a series of changing geometrical relationships. Where Greek astronomy attempted to create a geometrical model of the solar system by which to compute planetary positions, the Babylonians seem to have been content to measure time periods and to obtain positions by correctly combining time periods. Although the horoscope as we know it does seem to have some Babylonian antecedents, it was the Greeks who brought it to the form that we know. Although I realize many Hindu scholars might disagree with this statement, it appears that horoscopic astrology was brought to India from Greece. This is indicated by the large number of Greek astronomical terms in Hindu horoscopy. (There was undoubtedly a much older Hindu astrology that was non-horoscopic, which is not derived from Greek astrology.)

Because harmonics are divisions of periods of cosmic cycles, they are a more logical development to a people who approach astrology through time cycles rather than through geometrical structures. Also the Babylonians had a much greater involvement with number mysticism than did the Greeks. The well-known Pythagorean number mystics were strongly influenced by both Babylonian and Egyptian strains of thought. One can see Babylonian number mysticism as involved with time in the apocalyptic books of the Old and New Testaments. Here we find constant references to numbers that are significant because of astrological and astronomical associations. With this kind of an orientation, it would be simple to subdivide one sacred number by another to derive sacred and meaningful subdivisions.

We do not have any direct evidence that there ever was a sophisticated harmonic astrology in the ancient world. But it is instructive to note that in detail the Hindu works constantly refer to harmonic subdivisions that were once widely used but are no longer. These references date from the fifth century A.D. I know of no surviving works in India that describe the proper use of these subdivisions. This suggests that they were taken from somewhere else, especially when one considers that with a few exceptions the Hindu method of employing harmonics is basically related to a Greek geometrical approach.

Let us look at the thirteenth-harmonic type of dodekatemorion. The first division of every sign is the same as the sign that it is in, just as in the dwadasamsa. Until the latter part of the sign, most planets would be in the thirteenth and dwadasamsa of the same name. However, the thirteen subdivisions do not skip a sign at the end of a sign. The sign Aries contains thirteenths from Aries through to Pisces and back to Aries. Taurus goes from Taurus to Taurus, and so forth with each sign. It is easy to see how one could go from the thirteenth to the dwadasamsa by simply dropping the last thirteenth from each sign and stretching out the remaining divisions to fill up the space. Also if one looks at the method of computation it is easy to see how one could be corrupted into the other.

> The dwadasamsa type was computed as follows:
>   Given a longitude x degrees in a sign
>   Dwad. = 12x
> The thirteenth-harmonic type was computed as follows:
>   Given a longitude x degrees in a sign
>   13th = 12x + x

The difference is only the addition of the last x degrees. And the result of omitting the last x produces a result that is schematically elegant even if not elegant from a harmonic point of view.

The change from the thirteenth-harmonic system to the dwadasamsa also causes the following consequences. Twelve subdivisions in a sign divide evenly into thirds of a sign and fourths of a sign. If we divide Aries into three equal parts, we find that each third contains four dwadasamsas. And the first dwadasamsa of each division has the name of a fire sign. The first dwadasamsa of the first third of Aries is Aries. The first dwadasamsa of the second third of Aries is Leo, and the first dwadasamsa of the last third of Aries is Sagittarius. If we do the same thing with Taurus we find the thirds beginning with earth signs: Taurus, Virgo and Capricorn. We are deriving the rulerships of the decanates. This could be a coincidence except for one thing. The Hindus also divided the signs into fourths called chatturthamsas, and these worked in the same manner as decanates. Where decanates proceed according to triplicity, the chatturthamsas proceed by quadruplicities so that the four quarters of Aries begin with the cardinal signs: Aries, Cancer, Libra and Capricorn. And of course, the first dwadasamsa of each quarter has the same name as the quarter. I am suggesting that the whole scheme of rulerships in both the decanates and the chatturthamsas is derived from the dwadasamsa. Thus the three most significant departures from the general harmonic nature of the Hindu subdivisions of the zodiac appear to be traceable back to the one, the dwadasamsa, which in turn may be a corrupt form of the thirteenth-harmonic form of the dodekatemorion.

The Thirteenth Harmonic in Modern Astrology

With all of the activity in modern astrology concerning harmonics, one might expect the thirteenth harmonic to have been checked. It has been, by both me and John Addey and his associates. At first I thought, based on the symbolism of the number 13 in popular tradition, that the thirteenth harmonic might have something to do with death or something else similarly grim. And early work seemed to bear this out. However, more recently I have failed to be convinced. In the charts of a number of people with peculiar kinds of deaths, I have failed to find any symbolism in the thirteenth-harmonic charts that related to the nature of the death.

Since then, having discovered the thirteeth-harmonic dodekatemoria, I and others have begun to use the thirteenth harmonic in the same manner as the ancient Greeks. Here is the method.

First of all, compute the thirteenth-harmonic positions of each of the planets and the nodes. Do not compute the harmonic positions of the Ascendant and Midheaven. For those who might not be familiar with harmonic calculations, the method is covered in the last section of this article.

Place the thirteenth-harmonic positions into the conventional natal chart using some means to distinguish them from the normal first-harmonic positions. I recommend that the thirteenth-harmonic positions be put near the inside of the chart wheel. This is simply to prevent the chart from getting too cluttered and it also enables one to ignore the thirteenth-harmonic positions or to discriminate between them and the others whenever necessary.

Read all aspects among the thirteenth-harmonic positions as well as the interaspects between the thirteenth and the normal positions. This is similar to the conventional method of reading antiscia (solstice points). House positions of the thirteenth-harmonic positions in the first-harmonic houses appear to be significant, as well as the sign positions. In other words once you have computed the thirteenth-harmonic positions, you can forget that they are thirteenth-harmonic positions. It is just as if each planet had two positions.

While others have had slightly different experiences, I have not found that the thirteenth-harmonic positions tell a great deal that one could not have gotten from a thorough analysis of the conventional chart. However, the aspects within the thirteenth-harmonic positions and between them and the first-harmonic positions seem to heighten and emphasize the most important elements of the chart. It is like underlining or boldface print in a book. It does not add so much to the content as it makes it easier to see which parts of the contents are most significant. This is the reason why I recommend that the two types of positions be kept distinguishable from each other. Doing this will stop you from using the thirteenth-harmonic positions unnecessarily.

I must admit that there are charts in which the thirteenth harmonics do seem to indicate things that are not clear in the conventional chart, but I am suspicious of these. Whenever one adds positions to a horoscope, there is the danger that one will get meaningless indications simply because adding to the chart makes it easier to read whatever you desire into the chart. We must be very careful of this in connection with dodekatemoria. For this same reason I do not recommend using midpoints, Uranian pictures or any similar devices in connection with dodekatemoria lest one create a confusion of factors in which one could see anything. This is a technique that should be used for getting a large-scale overview of the chart, for finding out what is really important and what is not, not for doing detail work in the chart. Of course anything I say now is obviously preliminary.

But what I have just said almost inevitably follows for any technique that greatly increases the number of factors in the chart. At this point some examples are in order.

First Example

As the first example I would like to offer my own chart. Like most astrologers I often begin testing a new technique on my own chart. However, in this case it was actually quite a while before I tried this technique on my own horoscope. When I did, I was quite impressed by the results. My birth data are: December 5, 1942 at 7:30:11 P.M. EWT in Plainfield, N.J., 74 W 25, 40 N 37. My official birthtime was 7:31 P.M. so my rectification is quite slight. I was originally given the time as being "around" 7:30 P.M. and had rectified it myself to 7:30:11 before finding that my birthtime had been recorded on my birth certificate at 7:31 P.M. I find that the slight adjustment does seem to make the angle more sensitive to transits and directions.

Turning now to my chart, I drew it in the manner that I described earlier with the thirteenth-harmonic dodekatemoria around the inside and the conventional positions on the outside.

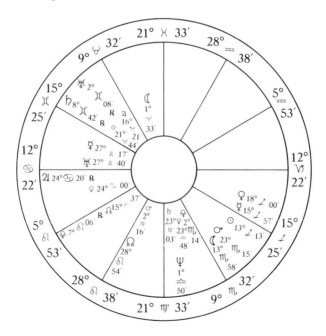

Figure 1. Robert Hand

In the past, one of the questions that has puzzled me about my chart is that it is not all that obvious that I am an astrologer from the chart, at least not if one limits oneself to the conventional forms of analysis in terms of signs, planets, houses and conventional aspects. I myself have always used midpoints extensively in my work. In my chart there is nothing in Aquarius; there are few aspects to my natal Uranus, unless you are inclined to large orbs; and the ones that exist are to other outer planets, which I would have in common with everyone else born in the same year. Using orbs of five degrees or less on major aspects, Uranus has only one aspect, the trine to Neptune, an aspect that was in effect for about five years. If one chooses to stretch orbs, one can see a conjunction with Saturn, but this too is with an outer planet. For those who like to use planetary nodes, my Sun is on the south node of Uranus. I feel that this is significant, not only because I am involved in astrology, but I am also very much involved in electronics and computer programming.

But the point remains that my astrological involvement is, at most, subtly indicated in my chart. But when one adds the dodekatemoria it becomes much more clearly emphasized. (From here on I will designate dodekatemoria by the letter D. Conventional positions will simply be indicated with no letter at all.) In the twelfth house (Koch) there is a conjunction between the Mercury(D) and Uranus(D). I have found Mercury-Uranus combinations, especially involving their midpoints, to be prominent in the charts of inventors, persons involved in electronics and computing and also among astrologers. The Saturn-Uranus conjunction in the first harmonic is reinforced by the square of Uranus(D) conjunct Mercury(D) to Saturn(D). Also the Sun-Saturn opposition in the first harmonic is reinforced by the trine between Sun(D) and Saturn(D).

There are many other possible examples of the effects of dodekatemoria that one could draw from my chart, but I would prefer to make the case for dodekatemoria more strongly from the charts of others. Suffice it to say that in my chart, as well as in the charts that follow, the reinforcing effect of dodekatemoria can be noted.

Second Example

My second example is Richard Nixon. I feel almost apologetic for once again trotting out a chart that has been over-examined by astrologers, including me, but that is precisely why I have chosen to do it again. Most astrologers are familiar with the chart. His data are January 9, 1913 at 9:35 P.M. PST in Yorba Linda, California, 117 W 49, 33 N 53. The time is from a note written by a nurse that has been reproduced photographically in several of Nixon's biographies. It is a well-authenticated birthtime.

The outstanding aspects in Nixon's chart in terms of his political career with its up and downs are the following (all referring to the first harmonic): Mars conjunct Mercury conjunct Jupiter, with all opposite Pluto. The conjunction is in the fourth house and Pluto is in the tenth.

This combination indicates a shrewd and resourceful mental fighter and debater, one who would not give up easily in a contest and who would resort to ruthless means, if necessary. The presence of the Jupiter makes it easy for him to be successful at it and also makes it likely that the effects of this combination of planets would express themselves in some kind of social or collective context (Jupiter as spokesman for the social order). The presence of the triple conjunction in the fourth house makes it clear that these energies in Nixon's psyche come from experiences in his earliest home life and were part of the forces by which he was nurtured. The opposition to Pluto in the tenth makes it also likely that these energies would be manifest in his career, being part and parcel from the very beginning of programming about how the social order works.

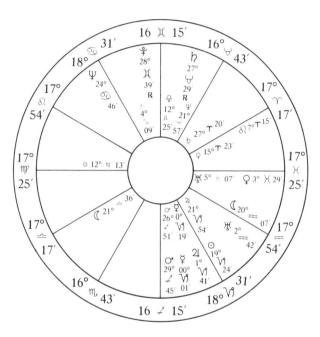

Figure 2. Richard Nixon

Sun opposition Neptune. This aspect is a bit wide, but for some reason was extremely active in the period in which Nixon fell from power. As readers of my book *Planets in Transit* are aware, this opposition falls near the meridian of his birthchart relocated to Washington, D.C. Most of the major crises during his fall from power occurred as the transiting Uranus squared either the Sun or Neptune or conjoined the Sun-Neptune midpoint. Of course, a Sun-Neptune opposition can indicate a weak reality system (as well as heightened sensitivities and receptivity) and a tendency to feel that one cannot be effective by applying one's energies in a straightforward manner. In his case the Sun is in the fifth house with Neptune in the eleventh. This suggests an unclear relationship between Nixon and the social collectives with which he would be associated throughout life. This manifests itself in Nixon's inability to express himself easily.

The Sun is the principle of self-expression in the sense of self-declaration; that is, it is an energy that declares to the world what kind of an entity one is. I have described the fifth house as the house in which one does what one does because of what one is, rather than because one has to. Thus we have two very strong self-expressive symbols weakened by the planet Neptune. Putting this into ordinary language we might say that this aspect says to the world, "I don't know who these people are around me. They do not inspire self-confidence. Therefore, it will be best if I do not show them who I am." But the mystery of this aspect is that it is not all that close, and yet it seems to have been very powerful in the Watergate period.

At any rate it is clear that these two aspect groupings were the most important in bringing about his fall from power. Do the dodekatemoria contribute anything to our understanding of these aspects? I believe they do.

In looking at the natal Mercury-Mars-Jupiter-Pluto combination we find that both Mercury(D) and Mars(D) are in about the same places in their dodekatemoria as they are in the first harmonic. This adds nothing to the symbolism, but seems to emphasize the importance of the combination, particularly its combative, verbal qualities. Saturn(D) trines and sextiles the combination from Sagittarius. This would seem to add structure and discipline to what could otherwise be a fairly explosive combination. Even so, Nixon did explode from time to time.

We get much more interesting material, however, when we turn to the Neptune-Sun combination. Moon(D) squares the Sun, Neptune, Jupiter(D), and opposes Saturn(D). Jupiter(D) conjoins the Sun and opposes Neptune(D) and squares Saturn(D). Venus(D), while out of orb of anything else, squares the Sun. Neptune(D) trines the Sun and Jupiter(D) and is quincunx to the Moon(D). Among other things, this last contact serves to repeat the symbolism of the first-harmonic Sun-Neptune opposition.

Admittedly this is a very complex combination of symbols. However, it does serve to explain some things about Nixon that are not extremely obvious in the conventional birth chart. For example, Nixon, though Republican, is not especially conservative. I doubt that he would have satisfied the party that nominated and helped elect Ronald Reagan. In foreign affairs he was decidedly liberal, opening the door to China. The presence of Jupiter(D) conjunct his Sun would help to explain that, although it might also be attributed to the Mercury conjunct Jupiter in the first harmonic.

I find the Moon(D)-Jupiter(D)-Saturn(D)-Neptune cross especially illuminating. Here we have in the Moon(D)-Jupiter(D) combination his ability to appeal to people (after all, one does not become president without any popular appeal); in Moon-Saturn, his having problems with his public image (Checkers, Watergate, etc.); in Moon(D)-Saturn(D)-Neptune(D) his image as "tricky"; and in Jupiter(D) square Saturn(D), his radical changes of fortune ("You boys won't have Dick Nixon to kick around any more").

Remember that the area of the chart in which this cross is located is the area transited by Uranus when his fortunes collapsed. In the first-harmonic chart it is a stressful area, but with the addition of the dodekatemoria it becomes really stressful.

Third Example

For our third case study I would like to offer Eleanor Roosevelt. It is particularly useful to look at her chart now that more is known about her personal life, especially her relationship with FDR. Ten years ago it would have been difficult to interpret some of the symbolism in her chart. Her birth data are from Joan Negus' beginner's books on astrology. Her source was family records and it appears to be reliable. We will assume that it is for the sake of this discussion. The data are October 11, 1884 at 11:00 a.m. EST in New York City, 40 N 45, 73 W 57.

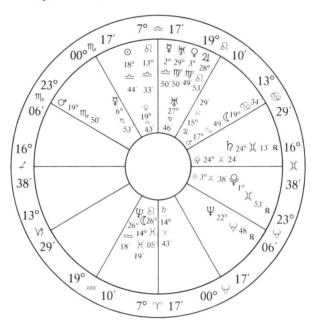

Figure 3. Eleanor Roosevelt

Her chart is of interest to me personally because I have spent some time reading about the Roosevelts. Also it was her chart that first got me interested in dodekatemoria. I was preparing a lecture on Ancient Greek and Hindu subdivisions in the zodiac to give to a National Council for Geocosmic Research meeting in San Francisco in the fall of 1980. I selected her chart as an example of dodekatemoria entirely out of the blue, simply to illustrate the technique. At that time I had no idea that it might turn out to be a useful technique. As I was lecturing it became clear both to me and to the audience that the dodekatemoria were telling us things about Eleanor Roosevelt. As I have said, I did not select her chart because the dodekatemoria worked. I honestly did not expect them to work. We were all surprised.

Marital difficulties are foreshadowed in her chart by means of Saturn in the seventh house in a wide (for my tastes) square to Uranus in the ninth. Also there is a Sun-Moon square in her chart, which usually signifies that the individual experienced the parents discordantly, one parent's influence seeming to push one way and the other parent's another way. In adults this often causes problems in marriage because one tends to reproduce the energies in one's own marriage that one perceived in the workings of the parents' marriage. Also the aspect indicates that the archetypal male and female energies are in a tense relationship within the self. The opposition of Mars to Neptune near the six-twelve cusp axis is especially interesting. This suggests a feeling of weakness and inferiority, of inadequacy and reluctance to face the world.

If one uses midpoints, another interesting pattern emerges. Note that the Sun-Mars angle is about the same as the angle between Saturn and Neptune, in both cases a slightly sloppy semisextile. A conventional astrologer might also note the wide quincunxes between the Sun and Neptune (about 4 degrees out of orb). To one used to midpoints, these orbs are a sign of a close midpoint aspect. If we calculate the midpoints we find that the midpoint Sun/Saturn is at 21 Leo 29 and the Mars/Neptune midpoint is at 21 Leo 19, an orb of 10 minutes from conjunction. This is an especially powerful combination because it links midpoints of two aspects in the natal chart, the wide Sun-Saturn trine and the closer Mars-Neptune opposition. The Sun is in the tenth, which is a house of fathering. This usually indicates that there was some kind of paternal energy that was strong and fairly powerful, giving the individual the need to emulate that person's success. In her case this was not her father, but her uncle, Theodore Roosevelt, one of the most powerful and popular presidents of the United States. But what of the tie-in between the Sun-Saturn and the Mars-Neptune? Sun-Saturn is the midpoint of fathering and being fathered. Tying it to Mars-Neptune makes it weak and not very effective. Her own father, Teddy's brother, Elliott Roosevelt, was a beautiful personality in many respects, according to his family, but an alcoholic, and a failure at just about everything he tried. One of her role models was Theodore and the other was Elliott. Both are shown in the chart.

Now to the dodekatemoria. With models like these she would be attracted to men of obvious strength and power. And, at the same time, she would tend to regard men as weak and needing to be taken care of. Even as a young man, FDR was obviously a dynamic and ambitious individual who would get somewhere. Her reaction to him was to admire him and take on the role of timid housewife. She regarded herself as a hopeless ugly duckling who by some miracle had gotten a catch like FDR.

Here is an interesting detail. As long as FDR was healthy and completely on his own, Eleanor played the classic nineteenth-century housewife role. Her husband had the limelight completely to himself while she bore and raised children. Then in the early 1920s, FDR was stricken with polio, which nearly killed him and made him a permanent cripple. All of a sudden FDR embodied both the weak and the strong male, physically weak, but with a strong personality. His handicap, coupled with the near death of their marriage because of the Lucy Mercer affair (betrayal by the male, another Mars-Neptune motif in female charts), caused Eleanor to move out on her own to become a world-renowned figure.

In the dodekatemoria we find Pluto(D) conjunct Saturn in the seventh. While this indicates possible great suffering in marriage, which she had, it also indicates that such suffering would be the agent of her own transformation. After the incident with Lucy Mercer was discovered, shortly after the end of the First World War, their marriage ceased to function sexually at all and became a largely platonic partnership.

Her eighth-house Moon is trine Mars near the cusp of the twelfth. This ties her Moon into the combination, giving back some of the strength that Neptune takes away. Mars(D) is conjunct her Moon, stating the same theme but more emphatically. Venus(D) squares the Mars(D)-Moon combination and conjoins the Sun. She was genuinely loved by her father, by Theodore Roosevelt and by FDR even though he sought sex elsewhere. The Venus(D) serves to mitigate the negative symbolism relating to males in the chart. Even though her sexual relationship with FDR appears to have ended in 1919, they worked together closely and harmoniously in later life, especially after the polio attack. She became his right hand.

The Moon conjunct Mars(D) trine Mars and square to Venus(D) conjunct Sun also reveals another peculiar aspect of her life, her ambiguous relations with other women. Other women were either very good friends or she had real problems with them. On one hand we have the almost lifelong struggle between her and FDR's mother, Sarah Delano Roosevelt, for influence over FDR (Sarah won that round). And on the other hand we have the close relationship between her and another woman in later life that some commentators have recently suggested was a homosexual relationship. That may or may not be so and probably is not, considering her upbringing, but both kinds of relationships with women are clearly shown in her chart with the addition of the dodekatemoria.

Saturn(D) is in the fourth indicating the difficulties that she had in childhood. With an alcoholic father she did not have the typical indulged upbringing of children of the upper classes of that time. The family was constantly in debt. This Saturn(D) is also opposite her Sun and Venus(D) as well as squaring her Moon and Mars(D). This adds another element to the theme of early difficulty emerging as difficulty within relationships. It is also interesting to note that many people have praised Eleanor Roosevelt's warmth and concern for humanity both individually and collectively:

Venus(D) conjunct Sun square Mars(D) and Moon. At the same time those close to her regarded her as rather cold (Saturn coming into the picture). Both these sides are clearly shown by the relationship of the dodekatemoria and the first-harmonic planets.

Conclusions—Why Thirteen?

It appears that the thirteenth harmonic is a kind of restatement of the first. That is why the Greeks were able to put dodekatemoria into their charts along with first-harmonic positions. But if this is true, why is it true? Thirteen is not a number that we think of as fundamental, not like ten, twelve or sixty. Insofar as it is encountered in tradition, it is as an evil number—thirteen persons at the last supper, Friday the thirteenth, etc. There is no simple answer to this question, and I do not expect to give an explanation that is truly satisfactory. The best that can be done is to offer some points that suggest an answer.

Thirteen is related to twelve as eleven is related to ten, that is to say, if a number system were based on twelve, instead of ten, thirteen would be the beginning of a second cycle of numbers. January is month thirteen following the previous January as month one. Counting middle C as one, the note C one octave higher is the thirteenth semitone. Addey in his work on harmonics seems to feel that the number system of harmonics is base ten with nine signifying completion. (Personally, using his logic, I would tend to think of ten as completing the cycle.) Perhaps this is an error. Maybe twelve is the base, in which case thirteen starts the next cycle. This is the quality of alpha and omega ("I am the Alpha and the Omega") in the thirteenth harmonic. All first-harmonic signs start and end with dodekatemoria that are of the same name as themselves. Aries begins and ends with Aries, Taurus with Taurus and so forth. Many consider twelve to be the basis of astrology. Maybe it is true of the harmonics as well as the signs and houses.

There is another curious quality about thirteen that should be mentioned. If you take thirteen spheres of equal size, twelve of them fit about the thirteenth so that the outer spheres all touch their neighbors perfectly as well as the sphere in the center.

This interesting fact also suggests a possible relationship between seven and thirteen. If, instead of spheres of equal size, one takes circles on the surface of a plane, then six circles around the outside touch a seventh circle in the center. Try it with coins and you will see. Thirteen is the three-dimensional analog of seven. Perhaps there is also a connection between the seventh and thirteenth harmonics.

Unfortunately, this is just speculation. We do not know at this time why thirteen should have any special quality with respect to harmonics, yet it seems to. I suggest that the best course is to try it out in practical use and see if it assists you in reading the chart. I think it might, and it is not a difficult set of calculations. It seems from what work has been done so far that the thirteenth-harmonic dodekatemoria may be a useful tool in deciding which symbols in a chart are important and which are not.

How to Compute Harmonic Positions

The general procedure for computing positions in any harmonic is the same. We will use the thirteenth here for obvious reasons.

The main tool required is a calculator. One can do these calculations by hand, but a calculator will increase the accuracy as well as the speed.

1. Convert all degrees and minutes to decimal degrees. To do so, divide the minutes of each position by 60, then add the resulting decimal to the degrees.
2. Reduce all positions to 360-degree notation. All longitudes should be expressed as so many degrees and minutes from 0 degrees of Aries rather than from the beginning of the particular sign. This is done by adding to the position in each sign the number from the table below.

Aries	0	Leo	120	Sagittarius	240
Taurus	30	Virgo	150	Capricorn	270
Gemini	60	Libra	180	Aquarius	300
Cancer	90	Scorpio	210	Pisces	330

3. Multiply all the resulting longitudes (expressed from 0 Aries) by the number of the harmonic, in this case 13.
4. Divide all of the above by 360 degrees. This will result in a mixed decimal for each.
5. Subtract the whole-number portion of each mixed decimal from the mixed decimal. Only a pure decimal fraction will be left.
6. Multiply the result by 360 again.
7. Convert the result back to degrees and minutes and express in conventional sign notation rather than 360-degree notation.

Example: Compute the dodekatemorion of Mars at 16 Libra 32.
  $16 + 32/60 = 16.533333$ or 16 Lib 32 = 16.533333 Lib
  Add 180 degrees for Libra. 196.533333 = 16.533333 + 180
  $196.533333 \times 13 = 2554.933333$
  $2554.933333/360 = 7.097037$
  $7.097037 - 7 = .097037$
  $.097037 \times 360 = 34.933333$
  34.933333 converts to 4 Tau 56.
The dodekatemorion of Mars at 16 Lib 32 is 4 Tau 56.

12

The Ascendant, Midheaven and Vertex in Extreme Latitudes

For the Ascendant and Midheaven, extreme latitudes are those near the poles. For the Vertex, extreme latitudes are those in the tropics in the midst of some of the most populated regions of the world. I say this to make it clear that the problems of these mundane points in extreme latitudes are not merely academic ones. And the problems that arise in defining and calculating all three of these points affect house division in the arctic, antarctic and tropics quite severely. Let me say at the outset that there are no house systems that are completely free of difficulties in these latitudes, not even the ones that are popularly so regarded. All house systems require an unambiguous definition of one or more of the Ascendant, Midheaven or Vertex and for all three there are latitudes where it is difficult to find such a definition.

Definitions

The definition of the Ascendant, Midheaven and Vertex may seem quite simple to the technically inclined astrologer, but it is a bit more complex than it looks even in "normal" latitudes. The Ascendant, Midheaven and Vertex are all nodes, i.e. points defined by the intersection of two great circles upon the celestial sphere. In this respect they are just like the nodes of the Moon. Charles Jayne repeatedly has pointed out that all simple sensitive points (excluding midpoints, Arabic Parts and the like) are either planets or nodes. Just as the Moon's Nodes are defined as the points where the great circle of the Moon's orbit intersect the great circle of the ecliptic, so the Ascendant, Midheaven and Vertex are defined as nodes of the ecliptic with the horizon, meridian circle and prime vertical. Which great circles define the Ascendant, Midheaven and Vertex distinguishes each from the other and determines whether they are ascending or descending nodes. For each of these points there is more than one definition, which in turn leads to different results in extreme latitudes. What follows is a brief list of pairs of definitions for the three sensitive points. Each definition leads to different consequences in extreme latitudes.

1. The Ascendant

    A. According to Direction: The intersection of the ecliptic and rational horizon in the east, i.e. the eastern node.
    B. According to Up and Down: The ascending node of the ecliptic upon the rational horizon.

2. The Midheaven

    A. According to Direction: The intersection of the meridian circle and the ecliptic in the south. This is expressed by the old English term "southing," used for upper meridian passes.
    B. According to Up and Down: The intersection of the meridian circle and the ecliptic that is above the horizon, as opposed to the one below the horizon, which in normal latitudes is the Imum Coeli (I.C.).

3. The Vertex

    A. According to Direction: The intersection of the prime vertical with the ecliptic in the west.
    B. According to Up and Down: The ascending node of the ecliptic on the prime vertical. Here the north point of the horizon defines up and the south point of the horizon defines down.

The Problems

In latitudes that are neither polar nor tropical, for the Ascendant, Midheaven and Vertex, both definitions in each pair are equivalent to the other. For this reason it has not occurred to most observers that it might be necessary to choose one from each pair as more applicable than the other. However, if we move to the Arctic (or Antarctic) things begin to change rapidly for the Ascendant and Midheaven. The following illustrations will reveal the nature of the problem.

Figure 1 is a graph of the longitudes of the Ascendant and Midheaven at 80° north as functions of sidereal time. The numbers across the top are hours of sidereal time. The Ascendant values employed in the graph are those derived directly from the standard formulas, which are given at the conclusion of this paper. In terms of the two definitions of the Ascendant given above, this is the second, i.e. the ascending node of the ecliptic upon the horizon, without respect to whether it may be in the east or west zone of the horizon. The Midheaven values that are used are also derived directly from the standard formulas (see following sections). These values assume that the Midheaven is always in the south without respect to whether the Midheaven is above or below the horizon.

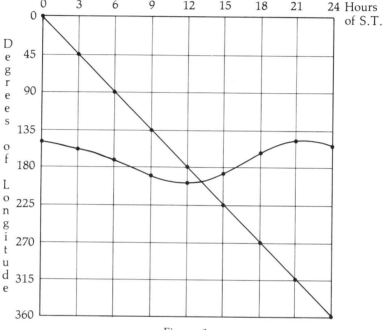

Figure 1.

Several peculiarities may be noted. First of all the Ascendant is always in Virgo or Libra, ranging from, 4° Vir 08' to 25° Lib 52'. The further one gets above the Arctic Circle, the nearer the Ascendant (defined as an ascending node) stays to 0° Libra. At the North Pole the Ascendant is always 0° Libra (again according to this definition).

And since the Ascendant value is always near 0° Libra, it must also, therefore, go backwards at some point as sidereal time increases, i.e. the longitude of the Ascendant will decrease as the longitude of the Midheaven increases. At 80° north this occurs from a sidereal time of about 13:36:00 until about 22:20:00. At both of these sidereal times the Ascendant is stationary, a characteristic normally associated only with planets.

Because the Ascendant is limited to a range of longitudes around 180 degrees while the Midheaven goes completely around the zodiac, this means that the M.C. must sometimes be below the horizon. Or does it? It depends upon definitions.

At the point where the Ascendant seems to go stationary retrograde (13:36:00 S.T.) the Midheaven conjoins the Ascendant. Speaking in terms of direction, the Ascendant moves from the eastern half of the horizon to the western half, because the Midheaven defines the boundary between east and west on the ecliptic. However, if the definition of the Ascendant is changed to define it as the eastern node of the ecliptic upon the horizon, then one can always have an Ascendant east of the Midheaven. But there is a twofold price to pay!

One has to be willing to have an Ascendant with a descending node of the ecliptic upon the horizon, and one has to be willing to accept a Midheaven that is below the horizon. Additionally, this causes a very strange thing to happen in the table of Ascendants for these latitudes. When the Midheaven longitude reaches that of the Ascendant, the longitude of the Ascendant must flip over 180 degrees in order to keep it east of the Midheaven, so that in an instant the Ascendant goes from conjunction with the Midheaven to an opposition.

Mathematically speaking, with this approach, the standard formula for the Midheaven will always produce the correct Midheaven. However, the Ascendant will have to be exchanged with the Descendant whenever the Ascendant is west of the Midheaven. But, we can take the other route. Let us define the Ascendant as the ascending node of the ecliptic upon the horizon, and the Midheaven as the node of the ecliptic upon the meridian that is above the horizon. In the case of the Ascendant we will not care whether it is east or west, and in the case of the Midheaven we will not care whether the Midheaven is in the south or the north, so long as it is above the horizon.

This seems more reasonable on the face of it. The term, Ascendant, implies an ascending node. Also because east and west become increasingly indistinct from each other as one approaches the Poles, until they become altogether meaningless at the Poles, having an Ascendant in the west is not as strange a thing as it would appear at normal latitudes. In addition, the Midheaven is not clearly an ascending or descending node, first because the angle between the ecliptic and meridian at the Midheaven is very nearly perpendicular compared to the angle between the ecliptic and the horizon, and second, because it is not at all clear which side of the meridian circle is up and which is down. The directions involved are left and right more clearly than up or down.

However, even with this change we still have a problem in the Midheaven. Prior to this, with the Ascendant in the east, we had to flip the Ascendant 180° when it reached the M.C. Here we have to flip the Midheaven 180° when it reaches the Ascendant. Therefore, the Midheaven instantly goes from a conjunction to an opposition in relation to the Ascendant. However, the rest of the time the Ascendant is always forward from the Midheaven in the zodiac. So whenever the Ascendant crosses over into the west, the Midheaven moves from the south to the north.

Mathematically speaking, the standard formulas for the Ascendant will always produce the correct Ascendant according to this second set of criteria. But the Midheaven resulting from the usual formula will have to be exchanged with the Imum Coeli whenever the calculated Midheaven is forward of the Ascendant in the zodiac. Both sets of formal definitions produce results that require mathematically inconsistent procedures.

With the Vertex we have the same problems in the tropics that we have with the Ascendant in the Arctic and Antarctic. This is due to the fact that the horizon at 80° north is the same as the prime vertical at 10° south. Recall that the prime vertical and the horizon are great circles that are always at right angles to each other. If we subtract 90° from 80° we obtain −10° or 10° south latitude.

If we define the Vertex as the intersection of the prime vertical and the ecliptic in the west, then we will have a Vertex at which the ecliptic goes south of the prime vertical (descending node) rather than north of the prime vertical as is usually the case in middle latitudes (ascending node). However, if we pick the ecliptic–prime vertical intersection according to whether it is an ascending node regardless of the direction, we will sometime get the Vertex in the east. Also, if we define the Vertex as an ascending node, it will, like the Ascendant at 80° north, oscillate around 0° Aries, going stationary and retrograde, then stationary and direct. This is because the Vertex at 10° south is opposition the polar Ascendant at 80° north.

Consequences for House Systems

All of the above indicates problems for the various systems of house division. These problems can be solved by choosing one or the other from each pair of possible definitions. However, astrologers have not done so. Here are some samples of the results of house cusp values for each of eight systems. The data are 80° north at an RAMC of 280°.

	10.	11.	12.	Asc.	2.	3.
Campanus	9°Cap11'	1°Can24'	15°Gem07'	22°Pis41'	28°Cap38'	16°Cap24'
Regiomontanus	9°Cap11'	24°Sco53'	17°Lib23'	22°Vir41'	2°Vir49'	10°Leo55'
Meridian	9°Cap11'	7°Aqu35'	8°Pis21'	10°Ari53'	12°Tau27'	11°Gem32'
Morinus	10°Cap53'	12°Aqu27'	11°Pis32'	9°Ari11'	7°Tau35'	8°Gem22'
Topocentric	9°Cap11'	18°Sag01'	28°Lib02'	22°Vir41'	21°Leo17'	25°Can01'
Alcabitius	9°Cap11'	13°Aqu06'	20°Pis22'	22°Vir41'	23°Tau32'	16°Gem43'
Porphyry	9°Cap11'	3°Ari41'	28°Gem11'	22°Vir41'	28°Leo11'	3°Leo41'
Equal	22°Gem41'	22°Can41'	22°Leo11'	22°Vir41'	22°Lib41'	22°Sco41'

All of these values are derived from standard formulas and assume that the Ascendant is the ascending node of the ecliptic upon the horizon. Koch (Birthplace System or GOH) and Placidus systems completely break down under these conditions and have been omitted.

Based on the ideal that houses ought to be somewhere near equal, only Equal houses, Morinus houses and Meridian houses make any sort of sense when looked at in this way. And equality of houses is not the only problem. It is also considered customary that the houses increase in longitude from the tenth-house cusp forward. Campanus, you will note, leaps all over the place. Partly this is due to the selection of a rigorous formula for Campanus that uses the direct solution of spherical triangles from the meridian to the horizon. This results in this formula producing an Ascendant that is always in the east but is sometimes a descending node. The other method, employing poles, would give an Ascendant of 22°Vir41'. But even with this we have the cusps running backwards.

Regiomontanus also runs backwards, along with Topocentric. However, Topocentric is not even this neat. If we take an RAMC of 273° and a latitude of 66° N 30' (which is south of the Arctic Circle by the way) we get the following interesting results.

$$\text{RAMC} = 273° \qquad \text{Latitude} = 66° \text{ N } 30'$$

	10.	11.	12.	Asc.	2.	3.
Topocentric	2°Cap45'	13°Cap04'	24°Can32'	28°Gem59'	13°Gem42'	22°Gem52'

After obligingly increasing from houses ten through twelve, the cusps begin to turn backwards until the third house, which is forward of two again. (Thanks to José Lebron and David Bennett for this example.) The Topocentric system is one of the few quadrant systems to break down below the Arctic Circle.

Meridian, Morinus and Equal houses produce somewhat more rational-looking results. However, Morinus and Meridian produce results very different from Equal. Of these, only Morinus is to some extent proof of the effects of extreme latitudes. This is because it uses neither the Ascendant, Midheaven nor Vertex as points of definition. Instead, an East Point is used as the cusp of the first house, and the tenth house is defined as always being in a particular direction, a definite number of degrees along the equator from the East Point. The first house of the Morinus system is not, however, the same as the first house of the Meridian system. It passes a great circle from the poles of the ecliptic through the East Point of the equator onto the ecliptic. As long as there is a clear definition of east, Morinus will work.

Meridian and Equal houses are both affected by the ambiguity of the Ascendant and Midheaven in the Arctic. Both, however, will work perfectly well as long as a standard definition of both of these points is agreed upon. Of course, Equal houses break down right on the Arctic and Antarctic circles when, once each day, the horizon perfectly coincides with the ecliptic. However, this occurs for only an instant and only on the infinitesimal band of the Arctic and Antarctic circles, so it is not a serious drawback in practice.

Alcabitius and Porphyry are quite badly deranged in the Arctic and Antarctic. Both go forward and then backward in longitude in our test case. This problem again arises from ambiguity of the definitions of the Ascendant and Midheaven. In both of these house systems the Ascendant and Midheaven are derived directly from the mathematical formulas. And, as we have already pointed out, deriving the Ascendant and Midheaven from purely mathematical formulas produces results that are incompatible with each other in the Arctic regions. This is the cause of the bizarre results in Alcabitius and Porphyry, but can be handled by accepting the Ascendant derived from the formula and calling the Midheaven 9°Can11' instead of 9°Cap11' as in the above tables. Then for Alcabitius we would have to add 180° to the longitudes of houses eleven and twelve as well. For Porphyry we would calculate new intermediate houses based on the Midheaven of 9°Can11' and the Ascendant of 22°Vir41'. In fact, however, these would be related to the ones in the table above. The new house eleven would be the old house three, the new house twelve would be the old house two, while the new houses two and three would be the old houses twelve and eleven respectively.

Referring back to Campanus and Regiomontanus, which came out backward, we can also make these behave by changing the designations of some of the houses. For Campanus we would have to change the Midheaven to 9°Can11' and the Ascendant to 22°Vir41'. This would put the Ascendant in its proper position as an ascending node and would put the Midheaven above the horizon. House eleven would be house three plus 180°; house twelve would be house two plus 180°; house two would be house twelve plus 180°; and house three would be house eleven plus 180°. For Regiomontanus, the Midheaven should also be changed by 180° and the houses exchanged in the same manner as Campanus.

By standardizing the definitions of the Midheaven and Ascendant so that one or the other definition in each pair is used consistently, we can overcome the difficulties of most house systems in the Arctic. As I have already said, I always favor making the Ascendant the ascending node of the ecliptic upon the horizon, and concurrently making the Midheaven the ecliptic-meridian intercept above the horizon. This sometimes necessitates reversing some of the other cusps, but these reversals do not violate the spirit of the mathematical bases of any of these systems. However, we must be prepared to have Ascendants in the west and Midheavens in the north. This situation should not be too hard to accept since Midheavens, at least, also occur in the north part of the sky south of the equator. In the tropics we must be prepared to accept a Vertex that is in the east instead of the west, because the horizon of the tropics is the prime vertical of the Arctic or Antarctic and vice versa.

Even below the Arctic Circle, the Topocentric system produces anomalous results that cannot readily be straightened out. This is due to its artificial mathematical nature. I suspect that this is a sign of the invalid nature of the system.

Koch and Placidus, which do not always yield a complete set of cusps in the Arctic and Antarctic, have logical bases that are quite different from the systems mentioned above. They certainly do not work in the Arctic and Antarctic, but it does not necessarily mean that they are invalid in all latitudes. In fact, there is a procedure for calculating house positions of planets right up to the poles in Placidus, even though there will not always be ecliptical cusps. Koch cannot be salvaged in extreme latitudes. I have to acknowledge that this same argument could be applied to Topocentric houses as well, but I think there is a difference between house systems that work consistently up to a point and then simply cannot be defined, versus ones that give cusps that are completely scrambled and cannot be rationalized by any means whatsoever. At the very least the Topocentric system gives inelegant results.

One final word on a house system that is not discussed here, the Horizontal system. This system is derived by dividing the horizon into twelve equal arcs by means of great circles dropped from the zenith to the nadir. As the horizon at $X°$ latitude is the same as the prime vertical at $X-90°$ latitude, Horizontal houses at $X°$ latitude are the same as Campanus houses at $X-90°$ latitude. Thus the Horizontal house system would have the same problems in the tropics that Campanus does in the Arctic, with the same solutions.

Standard Formulae Encountered in Astrology

The formulas given here are those that are necessary to repeat the investigations involved in this paper.

Section I: Calculations Pertaining to the Mundane Sphere

All of the calculations that follow are useful either preparatory to various systems of house division or for preparing specula for various kinds of primary directions.

1. To Convert Sidereal Time to a Degree on the Ecliptic. [This is most commonly used to find an M.C. but is also useful in the Placidus methods shown in Section II.]

   A. Convert sidereal time from hours, minutes and seconds to decimal hours.
      Dec. Hours = Hours + Minutes/60 + Seconds/3600
   B. Multiply sidereal time in decimal hours by 15 to convert to degrees of Right Ascension. This will be referred to as RAMC.
   C. Longitude = arctan(tan RAMC / cos obliquity of ecliptic)
   D. Alternate Formula:
      Longitude = arccot(cot RAMC × cos obliquity of Ecliptic)
   E. Quadrant Check: The longitude and RAMC should always be in the same quadrant.

   [Steps C & D are generally applicable wherever a degree in R.A. that has no celestial latitude must be converted to a longitude. In further formulae these often may be employed for this purpose.]

2. To Calculate an Ascendant, Given Sidereal Time and the Latitude of Birthplace. [This method is usually used only when the Ascendant itself is desired without other house cusps. Most systems of house

division have methods for calculating house cusps peculiar to themselves.]

A. Convert sidereal time to decimal degrees as in 1A & 1B, Section I.
B. Ascendant = arctan(cos RAMC/−[(tan latitude × sin obliquity)+(sin RAMC × cos obliquity)])
C. Quadrant Check: If the Ascendant is negative add 180°. If the value, cos RAMC, is negative add 180° to the Ascendant. If both are negative add 360° to the original Ascendant from B.
D. Alternate Method: Add 90° to the RAMC to get O.A. of Ascendant, then use #10 to convert to a longitude. (See #10.)

3. To Find the Declination of a Degree on the Ecliptic that Has a Celestial Latitude of 0°.

A. Decl. = arcsin(sin longitude × sin obliquity)

4. Calculation of the Vertex. [This method is usually employed when only the Vertex itself is desired without other mundane points or house cusps.]

A. Vertex = arctan(cos RAMC/[(cot latitude × sin obliquity)−(sin RAMC × cos obliquity)])
B. Quadrant Check: If the Vertex is negative, add 180°. If the value cos RAMC is negative, add 180° to the Vertex. If both are negative, add 360° to the Vertex.
C. Alternate Method: Use the formula for the Ascendant in #2 but for the latitude substitute −(90°−latitude) and for RAMC use RAMC + 180°.

5. To Find Ascensional Difference (Asc. Diff.).

A. Asc. Diff. = arcsin(tan decl. × tan latitude)

6. To Find Oblique Ascension or Descension.

A. Oblique Asc. = R.A.−Asc. Diff.
B. Oblique Desc. = R.A.+Asc. Diff.

7. To Find Diurnal and Nocturnal Semiarcs (D.S.A. and N.S.A.).

A. D.S.A. = 90° + Asc. Diff.
B. N.S.A. = 90° − Asc. Diff.

[In other texts there are two methods given for D.S.A. and N.S.A. depending upon whether north or south latitude. This is because the older texts were oriented toward calculation by logarithms in which the Asc. Diff. calculation (see #5) gave the absolute value of the Asc. Diff. Calculators and computers, however, give the signed value. In all cases the signed value of the Asc. Diff. as produced by #5 added to 90° for D.S.A. and subtracted for N.S.A. will give the correct result.]

8. To find the D.S.A. and N.S.A. of a Degree on the Ecliptic that Has a Celestial Latitude of 0°.

    A. Find the declination of the degree using #3.
    B. Find the semiarcs of the degree using #5 and #6.

9. To Find the Right Ascension of a Degree on the Ecliptic Having a Celestial Latitude of 0°.

    A. R.A. = arctan(tan longitude × cos obliquity)
    B. Quadrant Check: The R.A. and longitude should always be in the same quadrant.

10. To Convert an Oblique Ascension to a Longitude.

    A. X = arctan(tan latitude/cos O.A.)
    B. Y = X + obliquity
    C. Longitude = arctan(tan O.A. × cos X/cos Y)
    D. Quadrant Check: If longitude is negative add 180°. If the value sin O.A. is negative add 180° to longitude. If both are negative, then add 360° to longitude.

11. To Find the So-Called East Point or Equatorial Ascendant.

    A. Add 90° to the RAMC and use steps C or D and E of formula #1.

Section II: Formulae Pertaining to House Systems

In this section we will not go into the geometry of each system. There are a number of perfectly good references that do so. Here we shall give only the computation procedures.

1. Placidus Houses: First Method. [This first method is best for machine or calculator routines because it is highly accurate and arrives at its results using few iterations. This is a Newton-Raphson successive approximation technique developed by David Bennett. If there are valid cusps for a given RAMC in the Arctic, this method will find them. The second method given below, that of Hugh Rice, does not work so well in high latitudes.]

    A. Calculate Midheaven using formula in Section I, #1.
    B. Calculate Ascendant using formula in Section I, #2.
    C. R = −tan latitude × tan obliquity
    D. For 11th House: T = 1/3
    X(0)=0.0
    X(1)=180.0
    [Warning: it may be necessary to use X(0)=.0000001 and X(1)=180.0000001 so as not to create problems with trig functions on some computers and calculators.]
    Y(0)= R × sin [RAMC + T × X(0)] − cos X(0)
    Y(1)= R × sin [RAMC + T × X(1)] − cos X(1)

E. $X(2) = X(1) - ([(X(1) - X(0)]/[Y(1) - Y(0)]) \times Y(1)])$
$Y(2) = R \times \sin [RAMC + T \times X(2)] - \cos X(2)$
Now give X(0) the value previously held by X(1), Y(0) the value previously held by Y(1), X(1) the value held by X(2), and Y(1) the value previously held by Y(2) and then repeat E.
Do so until the difference between X(1) and X(2) is within the desired approximation. Then proceed to next line.
R.A. of House Cusp = RAMC + X(2)
To convert the Right Ascension of the House Cusp to Longitude of the Zodiac, use the formula in Section I, 1C through 1E.

F. For Other Houses: The procedure is the same except for the following changes:
For 12: T = 2/3: R.A. of H.C. = RAMC + X(2)
For 2: T = −2/3: R.A. of H.C. = RAMC + X(2) + 180°.
For 3: T = −1/3: R.A. of H.C. = RAMC + X(2) + 180°.

2. Placidus Houses: Second Method. [This method is as accurate as the first, although it does not do so well in the Arctic and Antarctic. Its advantage for calculators is that it requires fewer variables than the above, but it also takes much longer. This is the method developed by Hugh Rice and used in the *American Astrology Table of Houses.*]

A. Calculate the M.C. and Ascendant as above.
B. For 11th House:
RA(0) = RAMC + 30°.
R = 3.0
X = arccos(−sin RA(0) × tan obliquity × tan latitude)
R.A.(1) = RAMC + (X/F)
Then replace R.A.(0) with the value of R.A.(1) and generate a new value of R.A.(1). Continue this until R.A.(0) and R.A.(1) are as close as desired.
Then convert R.A.(1) to longitude using formula from Section I, #1.
C. For other houses use the same procedure with the following changes:
For 12: R.A.(0) = RAMC + 60° : F = 1.5: R.A.(1) = RAMC + (X/F).
For 2: R.A.(0) = RAMC + 120° : F = 1.5: R.A.(1) = RAMC + 180° − (X/F)
For 3: R.A.(0) = RAMC + 150°: F = 3.0: R.A.(1) = RAMC + 180° − (X/F)

3. Placidus Houses: Third Method. [This and the following are not as accurate as the two above, but are sufficiently accurate for rough and ready work. This is the method used by Dalton.]

A. Calculate M.C. and Asc. as in previous case.
B. Calculate poles of houses.
Calculate Decl. of Longitude 52.00° on the ecliptic using formula from Section I, #3.

Calculate Asc. Diff. of that declination using formula from Section I, #5, for the geographic latitude in question.

Pole of 11 & 3 = arctan[sin(Asc. Diff./3)/tan Decl.]

Pole of 12 & 2 = arctan[2 × sin(Asc. Diff./3)/tan Decl.]

C. Calculate Oblique Ascensions of House Cusps (O.A.H.C.)

O.A.H.C. of 11 = RAMC + 30°.

O.A.H.C. of 12 = RAMC + 60°.

O.A.H.C. of 2 = RAMC + 120°.

O.A.H.C. of 3 = RAMC + 150°.

D. Convert the O.A.'s to longitude using formula in Section I, #10.

4. Placidus Houses: Fourth Method. [This is also an approximate technique that is probably not as good as the Dalton technique. It was used by the English, such as Leo, Sepharial, Zadkiel and Raphael. The Dalton method was supposed to be a reform of the following method.]

A. Proceed exactly as in #3 except use declination = obliquity for the calculation of the Asc. Diff.

5. Koch Houses: Also Known As Birthplace House System. [This technique is related to Placidus and Alcabitius (see below) in that semiarcs are divided according to some method. However, the results in the intermediate cusps can be quite different.]

A. Calculate Asc. Diff of the M.C. (ADMC).

ADMC = arcsin(sin RAMC × tan obliquity × tan latitude)

B. Calculate Oblique Ascension of M.C. (OAMC)

OAMC = RAMC − ADMC

C. Calculate diurnal semiarc of M.C. (DSAMC)

DSAMC = 90° + ADMC

D. Arc = DSAMC/3

E. Calculate O.A. of other houses.

O.A.(11) = OAMC + Arc

O.A.(12) = OAMC + 2 × Arc

O.A.(1) = OAMC + 3 × Arc

O.A.(2) = OAMC + 4 × Arc

O.A.(3) = OAMC + 5 × Arc

F. Convert all of above O.A.'s to longitude using the formula in Section I, #10.

[One could calculate the M.C. and Asc. using the conventional methods described above, but this method allows one to use a single procedure for all house cusps.]

6. Campanus Houses: First Method Using Poles. [Campanus does not gracefully adapt itself to using poles, but the use of poles allows for use of some of the same methods for Campanus that could be used for

Dalton-Placidus and for several other systems such as Regiomontanus and Topocentric (see below).]

A. Calculate poles of houses
Pole of 11 & 3 = arcsin(sin latitude × sin 30°)
Pole of 12 & 2 = arcsin(sin latitude × sin 60°)

B. Calculate the Meridian distance of the Polar Arcs, (MDP)
MDP of 11 & 3 = arctan[1/(cos latitude × tan 30°)]
MDP of 12 & 2 = arctan[1/(cos latitude × tan 60°)]

C. Calculate Obl. Asc. of house cusps (OAHC)
OAHC of 11 = RAMC + MDP of 11
OAHC of 12 = RAMC + MDP of 12
OAHC of 2 = RAMC + 180° − MDP of 2
OAHC of 3 = RAMC + 180° − MDP of 3

D. Calculate M.C. and Asc. using usual methods.

E. Convert OAHC's to longitude using formula from Section I, #10.

7. Campanus Houses: Second Method Without Poles. [This method is faster and takes up less machine space on a computer, but does not allow a Campanus routine to share any routine with other house systems.]

A. Calculate M.C. and Asc. by usual methods.

B. Calculate angle of meridian to ecliptic clockwise from zenith.
X = arccos(sin obliquity × cos RAMC)
If X is negative add 180°.
If X is greater than 180° subtract 180° from X.

C. Calculate value D.
D = arctan [1/(tan obliquity x sin RAMC)]

D. Find the interval on the ecliptic from M.C. to house cusp.
For 11th, A = 30°.
For 12th, A = 60°.
For 2nd, A = 120°.
For 3rd, A = 150°.
B = 1/tan A
C = D + latitude
Angle = arctan[sin C/(cos C × cos X + sin X × B)]

E. House Cusp = Angle of house + M.C.

8. Regiomontanus Houses.

A. Calculate M.C. and Asc. by usual methods.

B. Calculate Poles
Pole of 11 & 3 = arctan(tan latitude × sin 30°)
Pole of 12 & 2 = arctan(tan latitude × sin 60°)

C. Proceed exactly as in Dalton-Placidus, #3-C&D, Section II, to calculate O.A. of houses and convert them to longitudes.

9. Topocentric Houses.

   A. Proceed exactly as with Regiomontanus except calculate the poles according to the following procedure.
   Pole of 11 & 3 = arctan(tan latitude/3)
   Pole of 12 & 2 = arctan(2 × tan latitude/3)

10. Meridian Houses. [This is simply twelve equal houses on the equator projected onto the ecliptic using hour circles. This system is also known as Zariel and Axial. Meridian houses may also be computed by using Koch, Placidus, Regiomontanus or Campanus with a geographic latitude of 0°.]

    A. Calculate the R.A. of the houses.
    R.A. of 10 = RAMC
    R.A. of 11 = RAMC + 30°
    R.A. of 12 = RAMC + 60°
    R.A. of 1 = RAMC + 90°
    R.A. of 2 = RAMC + 120°
    R.A. of 3 = RAMC + 150°
    [Note: the first house cusp will not usually coincide with the Asc.; to get the Asc. use formula #2, Section I.]
    B. Convert all of the above R.A.'s to longitudes using formula #1, Section I.

11. Alcabitius Houses. [In only slightly altered form, this is one of the oldest systems known. It is found in Greek horoscopes of the Roman era. This is another semiarc system. The alteration found in the Greek manuscripts is that the houses are considered to begin 5° back clockwise from what most modern astrologers would consider to be the cusps. Thus, for example, the first house would begin 5° of R.A. back into the twelfth from the Ascendant. What we call cusps were not the beginning of the houses.]

    A. Calculate M.C. and Asc. in usual manner.
    B. Find the Diurnal and Nocturnal Semiarcs of the Ascendant using the formula found in #8, Section I.
    C. X = D.S.A./3
    D. Y = N.S.A./3
    E. Find R.A. of cusps
    R.A. of 10 = RAMC
    R.A. of 11 = RAMC + X
    R.A. of 12 = RAMC + 2X
    R.A. of 1 = RAMC + 3X
    R.A. of 2 = RAMC + 3X + Y
    R.A. of 3 = RAMC + 3X + 2Y
    F. Convert all of the R.A.'s to longitudes using the formula from #1 of Section I.

G. To get beginnings of Greek houses, simply subtract 5° from all of the house R.A.'s above, before converting to longitudes.

12. Porphyry Houses. [This is another system that was definitely used in the Roman period. In conception it is similar to Alcabitius but it trisects arcs on the ecliptic rather than the equator, and is, therefore, very easy to implement.]

A. Calculate the M.C. and the Asc. in the usual way.
B. $X = $ (Ascendant $-$ M.C.)/3
C. $Y = $ (I.C. $-$ Ascendant)/3
D. Longitude of 11 = M.C. + X
E. Longitude of 12 = M.C. + 2X
F. Longitude of 2 = M.C. + 3X + Y
G. Longitude of 3 = M.C. + 3X + 2Y

13. Morinus Houses. [To the best of my knowledge Morinus never used this system. He used Regiomontanus. I do not know what connection there is between Morinus and this system, but this is the name by which it has come down to us. Its outstanding peculiarity is that the M.C. is not the cusp of the tenth nor is the Asc. the cusp of the first. Instead we have two new points called the Midequator, which is the cusp of the tenth, and the East Point, which is the cusp of the first. To make matters worse, this East Point is not the same point as the cusp of the Meridian first house, which is also called East Point, and is also known as the Equatorial Ascendant.]

A. Calculate R.A.'s of the houses as in #10, Section II, Meridian Houses.
B. Convert each R.A. to longitude using the following formula.
Longitude = arctan(tan R.A. $\times$ cos obliquity)

13

The Age and Constellation of Pisces

The essay that follows is essentially a commentary on chapters 6-9 of Jung's book *Aion*. I say this to make it clear that the ideas are not wholly my own but have been inspired by one of the greatest prophetic minds of our time. It is also worth mentioning that a good deal of material contained in this part of *Aion* is inspired by Nostradamus. I say this only to indicate that what follows has quite a lineage. The conclusions that I draw from the material presented herein are largely my own.

The Morphomata

Constellations have not played much of a role in modern astrology. Fixed stars taken individually have been investigated from time to time, but not usually as parts of constellations. Of course, there are the practitioners of sidereal astrology, both in the West and in India, who use signs that correspond to the constellations. That is, the sidereal sign Aries coincides roughly with the constellation of Aries, but this is not quite the same as a direct use of the constellations. The signs of the sidereal zodiac are twelve signs of equal extent. Each consists of 30 degrees exactly, but the actual constellations are of unequal extent.

The ancients made a distinction between two kinds of zodiacal sign, the *zodia noeta*, which roughly translates as the "knowable zodiac," and the *morphomata*, "that which has form." The zodia noeta consist of the constellations as the siderealists use them, twelve 30-degree sidereal signs. The morphomata (morphomaton in the singular), however, are the unequal constellations forming pictures of *forms* in the heavens.

The ancients used the sidereal signs (zodia noeta) for measuring purposes, to locate planets among the fixed stars. They may have also used them as modern astrologers use signs, as zones of influence affecting planetary energies that lie within them. But they do not seem to have used them in this way very extensively. The surviving works of the ancient astrologers place considerable emphasis on the groupings of fixed stars in the morphomata, both on and off the ecliptic. Ptolemy in both the *Almagest* and *Tetrabiblos* paid a great deal of attention to the morphomata. In the *Tetrabiblos*, Ptolemy's work on astrology, it is not clear whether he discusses the constellations of the zodia noeta (the twelve idealized constellations of 30 degrees) or the twelve zodiacal morphomata. To make matters worse, it is not even clear whether he intended the reader to apply his statements to the sidereal or tropical zodiac, because at the time of his writing the two zodiacs were extemely close.

However, in both works he refers to the parts of the morphomata as particular star groupings to which he assigns planetary influences in the *Tetrabiblos*. In the *Almagest* he gives the most complete descriptions of the arrangement of the stars into the various parts of the morphomata. We do not know to what extent his descriptions are traditional or of his own creating. But given the fact that most of Ptolemy's work was derived from earlier sources, we can assume that this is the case here as well as in the rest of his work. His descriptions have formed the basis of most descriptions of the constellations from his day to this. A star globe of modern manufacture in my possession has the constellations outlined on it precisely according to Ptolemy.

But while the constellations (morphomata) have retained their form fairly consistently from somewhat before Ptolemy to the present, it is quite apparent that they were different before that time. Most of the zodiacal constellations had the same name that they have now, but their physical shape among the fixed stars was somewhat different. At some point prior to Ptolemy there was only one fish in the constellation of Pisces. We do not know precisely when Pisces became two fish, because for some time both the single and double fish representation appear to have been used. Even as late as the Middle Ages when Al-Biruni wrote his work *Elements of Astronomy*, which included astrology, he could state that in most languages the word for Pisces signified only one fish. It is probable, however, that by the time of Hipparchus, the two-fish mode of representation had become standard at least in the West and Middle East.

Projection and Synchronicity

Before we proceed any further, there are some basic ideas that must be understood. Everything that will be said about the relationship of the movement of the vernal point through the constellation of Pisces (the morphomaton, that is) will be stated in terms of an acausal relationship. The presence of certain astronomical relations is not considered as causing anything. Rather these are signs or signatures of events in the evolution of consciousness. The constellation of Pisces does not signify events because of "radiation" from the fixed stars that constitute it. Instead, the constellation of Pisces takes on the form that it has because consciousness is ready to project upon it a particular drama. The drama occurs within the psyche of each person alive at the time of its occurrence. The effect of this in every person operates cumulatively to produce a cultural effect. In turn, the culture, being a collective event, keeps the psychic dimension of the drama alive from generation to generation, from individual to individual. The perception of Pisces, or any other celestial signature, is created by what transpires within the culture. Because certain things are happening within us, we see the world in certain ways, which tends to reinforce the events occurring within us, and so forth.

No causation is involved, yet the form of the physical universe evolves in a way that is parallel to the form of the psychic universe within us. We create our universe, which in turn recreates us in its image of our image. Synchronicity is essentially the result of a feedback loop between the psyche and the physical universe as the psyche perceives it.

The result of this is that we operate as if the physical universe causes the changes within. Individuals at any time in history do not have to know personally about the changes in the physical universe which reflect the evolution of consciousness in nature. For the individual, the process is largely unconscious, yet the individual participates in the collective process of projection, which is reflected in the symbolism in nature.

Let us be more concrete. Pisces as a constellation represents nothing as a reality that modern science could accept. The stars involved are not physically associated; that is, they are not members of a particular star-group. Nor do the stars involved even trace a clear image of two fish. Very few of us looking at the sky in the direction of Pisces or any other constellation are likely to see shapes suggesting the classical images of the morphomata. The stars of Pisces are particularly faint. Near most cities or with any degree of fog or air pollution they are invisible. The forms of Pisces and the other constellations come about because they symbolize mythic archetypes that represent the evolution of consciousness that is about to take place. They then keep that form until the evolution is concluded. On the historical level such a conclusion would be perceived as a complete breakdown of a culture, so that it could no longer be perceived as a driving force in history.

What makes Pisces unique? Since a little before the birth of Christ the backwards motion of the vernal equinox has been carrying it through the constellation of Pisces. Somewhere about the time the vernal point entered Pisces, Pisces became two fish having a certain peculiar relationship to each other. Since that time to the present, in the West at least, the form of the constellation has been constant. The presence of the vernal point in Pisces means that spring, the archetypal beginning of the year, takes place when the Sun is in Pisces. This is what is meant by the Piscean Age, although when we look at the morphomaton of Pisces rather than the astrological sign of the zodia noeta, either tropical or sidereal, we get a very different picture of the Piscean Age than we get from New Age literature.

The Morphomaton of Pisces

The actual constellation (morphomaton) of Pisces, as described by Ptolemy, consists of a pair of fish. The eastern fish, the one with greater longitude, swims vertically off the ecliptic. The western fish swims horizontally more or less parallel to the ecliptic. The two fish are tied together at the base of their tails by two cords that end in a knot south of the eastern fish. The symbol clearly reflects two energies that work at cross purposes with each other and are in a state of conflict. The star chart of Pisces (figure 1) reveals the arrangment of the stars. The tail of the eastern fish is Rho Piscium with the head at 65, 67 and 68 Piscium. The stars Eta, Pi and Omicron Piscium are the cord tying the eastern fish to the knot at Alpha Piscium. From Alpha to 41 Piscium extends the cord of the western fish. The tail of the western fish is at Omega Piscium with the mouth of the western fish at Beta Piscium. Beta Piscium is the last star of Pisces measuring westward from the beginning of the constellation, the direction in which the vernal point moves along the ecliptic. Although there is individual symbolism attached to some of the other fixed stars, it is not necessary for our purposes to go into it.

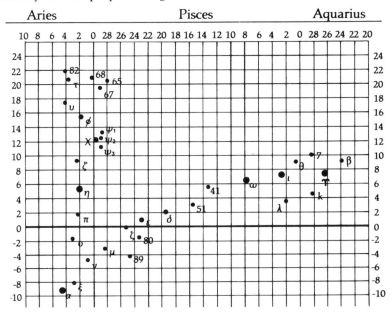

Figure 1.

The Chronology of the Precession Through Pisces

In order to examine the precession of the vernal equinox through Pisces, it is necessary to compute the dates at which it arrives at the longitude of the various fixed stars in the constellation. To do this I have converted the longitudes of the stars from the tropical to the sidereal zodiac. In the sidereal zodiac the only movement of fixed stars that occurs is due to the very slow proper motion of the stars. The sidereal positions have then been corrected for proper motion for the epoch 221 A.D., the era when the tropical and sidereal zodiacs corresponded. For this purpose I have adopted the values for the sidereal zodiac given by Fagan and Bradley. Scholars quite independent of Fagan and Bradley have deduced that the original Babylonian zodiac was close to the values derived by Fagan and Bradley.

The next procedure was simply to produce an ephemeris of the moving vernal point in the sidereal zodiac. Given this ephemeris and the table of fixed star positions, both of which are supplied with this paper, it is easy to compute the approximate year at which the vernal equinox comes to each fixed star. In tropical terms these are the dates at which each star reaches the longitude 00 Ari 00 00. Because of proper motion before and after 221 A.D. these dates are only approximately correct. However, they are sufficiently accurate (plus or minus a year) for our purposes.

Stars in the Constellation Pisces According to Ptolemy

	Ptolemy's Designation	Modern	Sid. Long.	Lat.	V.P.
West	Mouth of W. Fish	Beta	23 Aqu 54	9 N 08	2813 A.D.
Fish	South of 2 in Head	Gamma	26 Aqu 24	7 N 26	2635 A.D.
	North of 2 in Head	7	28 Aqu 18	8 N 56	2499 A.D.
	West of 2 in Back	Theta	00 Pis 33	9 N 03	2337 A.D.
	East of 2 in Back	Iota	2 Pis 46	7 N 15	2180 A.D.
	West of 2 in Belly	Kappa	28 Aqu 09	4 N 31	2510 A.D.
	East of 2 in Belly	Lambda	1 Pis 57	3 N 28	2237 A.D.
	Tail of West Fish	Omega	7 Pis 49	6 N 26	1817 A.D.
West	First Star in Cord	41	13 Pis 15	5 N 26	1427 A.D.
Cord	Second Star in Cord	51	15 Pis 26	3 N 08	1270 A.D.
	First of 3 Bright Ones	Delta	19 Pis 23	2 N 09	986 A.D.
	Next of 3 Bright Ones	Epsilon	22 Pis 49	0 N 59	739 A.D.
	Last of 3 Bright Ones	Zeta	25 Pis 05	0 S 15	576 A.D.
	Northern of 2 Little	80	23 Pis 19	1 S 32	703 A.D.
	Southern of 2 Little	89	24 Pis 36	4 S 21	612 A.D.
	West of 3 After Bend	Mu	28 Pis 15	3 S 05	348 A.D.
	Next of 3 After Bend	Nu	0 Ari 45	4 S 48	167 A.D.
	East of 3 After Bend	Xi	2 Ari 44	8 S 03	24 A.D.
Knot	Star in the Knot	Alpha	4 Ari 35	9 S 10	111 B.C.
North	First Star in N. Cord	Omicron	2 Ari 58	1 S 42	7 A.D.
Cord	Next in N. Cord	Pi	2 Ari 12	1 N 45	62 A.D.
	Third in N. Cord	Eta	2 Ari 05	5 N 17	71 A.D.

	Ptolemy's Designation	Modern	Sid. Long.	Lat.	V.P.
East	Tail of East Fish	Rho	2 Ari 23	9 N 16	49 A.D.
Fish	North of 2 in Mouth	82	4 Ari 08	21 N 54	77 B.C.
	South of 2 in Mouth	Tau	3 Ari 38	20 N 39	41 B.C.
	East of 3 in Head	68	0 Ari 14	20 N 52	204 A.D.
	Next of 3 in Head	67	29 Pis 04	19 N 24	290 A.D.
	West of 3 in Head	65	27 Pis 56	20 N 27	371 A.D.
	Binary in S. Fin	Psi 1	28 Pis 44	13 B 17	315 A.D.
	Next One in S. Fin	Psi 2	28 Pis 56	12 N 27	299 A.D.
	Last One in S. Fin	Psi 3	28 Pis 56	11 N 13	299 A.D.
	North of 2 in Belly	Upsilon	4 Ari 06	17 N 22	75 B.C.
	South of 2 in Belly	Phi	1 Ari 46	15 N 25	94 A.D.
	Star in East Fin	Chi	29 Pis 49	12 N 21	235 A.D.

This list groups the stars of Pisces according to structural relationships in the morphomaton, not according to longitudes or right ascensions. The years of the V.P. transit are approximate. The sidereal longitudes are as of 221 A.D., the year in which the tropical longitudes coincided with the sidereal zodiac.

Here are the major dates in the evolution of the Piscean Age as defined by the morphomaton:
1. 111 B.C. Alpha Piscium. The first star in Pisces to be encountered by the vernal point. This presumably defines the beginning of the age.
2. 371 A.D. 65 Piscium. This is the westernmost star in the eastern fish. This ends the era of the eastern fish.
3. 1351 A.D. The exact halfway point of the movement of the vernal point through the morphomaton.
4. 1817 A.D. Omega Piscium. The easternmost star of the west fish. The age of the west fish begins. From 371 to 1817 the vernal point moved along the cord connecting the knot (Alpha) to the tail of the west fish (Omega).
5. 2813 A.D. Beta Piscium. The mouth of the western fish and the westernmost part of the constellation of Pisces.

Symbolic and Historical Correlations

The Piscean Age has traditionally been considered the age of Christianity, at least as far as the West has been concerned. There is also reason to believe that the symbolism actually affects even those parts of the world that lie outside of the West, but this is only in modern times and is only the result of their encountering Western civilization. It has also only been in the West that the morphomaton has had precisely the form that I have just described, so we are justified in saying that this form represents the projection of the psychic, collective energy of the West only, until modern times. In the non-Western world, the Islamic nations have also shared the Western image of Pisces due to the fact that the Islamic world has shared equally in the heritage of ancient Greece and Rome. However, this does not contradict what has just been stated. We shall see that for our purposes, the world of Islam is operationally part of the Western sphere of culture.

Now let us ask what did happen on or about 111 B.C.? Was there anything that suggested a major change in world history? I think that we can say the answer is yes. However, we must remember that precession is a very slow process. It takes 72 years to move one degree. Therefore, we should not be looking for an event that occurs precisely at 111 B.C. What we should expect is a gradual process, not a sudden event.

When we examine this period we find that it is a period of intense religious ferment. In fact it foreshadowed, a century before Christ, the ferment that ultimately produced Christianity. The Essenes who produced the Dead Sea Scrolls were already on the scene as well as other similar groups such as the Therapeutae, who lived in monastic communities much like the Essenes and possessed a mystical-spiritual world-view not unlike Christianity.

Messianism of various kinds was already a major element in these religions. This ranged from the mainstream Jewish religion that expected a descendant of David to reestablish the old Jewish empire to the Essenes with their "teacher of righteousness." There is even evidence of a Christlike teacher who did come at about 100 B.C. and was stoned to death by the Jews.

Most important for our purposes, however, there was a sense that this was a pivotal and culminating time of history. It was generally believed that the old order was about to pass away and that divine judgment was at hand. This was a different kind of religion than the traditional paganism of the Greco-Roman world. It saw history as a stage upon which a tremendous drama of fall and redemption was being enacted. Although Christians usually think of these ideas as being peculiarly Christian, they actually precede Christianity.

The idea of history as a linear progression from Creation to Fall and then redemption (of at least an elect) was not new at this time. It is first seen in Zoroastrianism, the religion of the ancient Persians. The Zoroastrians saw history as a battle between the powers of light and darkness in which darkness had temporarily taken over this world. They believed that the forces of light would eventually win out, after which the world as we know it would come to an end.

The Jews in the time of the Babylonian captivity had come to know Zoroastrianism when they encountered the religion of the Persians, who conquered the Babylonians. The Jews regarded Ahura Mazda, the Zoroastrian god of light, as being identical with Jahweh, their own traditional god. They took many elements from Zoroastrianism, including the idea of the final battle between good and evil, and also reinforced their own view of history as the manifestation of the will of God on earth. Satan as an archangel of evil comes from this period. He is neither more nor less than a variation on Ahriman or Angra Mainyu, the Zoroastrian god of evil and darkness.

Zoroaster and this early Zoroastrianized Judaism precede the beginning of the Piscean Age by hundreds of years. However, the ideas embodied in these religions were confined to only two peoples, the Persians and the Jews. Then in the fourth century B.C. the Persians were conquered by Alexander, who allowed Zoroastrianism to flourish. However, the rulers who followed Alexander quickly lost their grip on the Persian part of the empire. It was conquered by the Parthians, a people of similar ethnic origin to the Persians, but who were not Zoroastrians. Under the Parthians, Zoroastrianism went underground, although it did not die out by any means.

The Jews did not fall to the Parthians. They remained under the rule, at least indirectly, of the Seleucid successors of Alexander, but one of them, Antiochus IV, attempted to suppress Judaism. The Jews revolted under the Maccabees and restored some measure of independence (168-164 B.C.). Thus the Jews managed to keep their traditions alive.

Also, the Jews had begun to spread out throughout the Mediterranean world. They developed an especially active community in Alexandria, Egypt. There in the third century B.C. a Greek translation was made of the religious writings of the Jews, what we call the Old Testament.

From there, the Jews dispersed all over the Mediterranean basin. Jewish thought combined with mystical traditions of other Eastern peoples spread throughout what was becoming the Roman world. Everywhere there were groups of people retiring to the desert and seeking to attain spiritual perfection, awaiting the arrival of a perfect master, messiah or teacher of righteousness. Many of these people were in Palestine and Egypt. By 111 B.C. these ideas had spread all over the Western world of the time, paving the way for Christianity. But before we continue let us briefly summarize the main points about what made the new religious concepts unique.

First of all, there was a new view of history. The more ancient religions had viewed the world as an endless series of creations and destructions, a view to be found to this day in Hinduism. In the new religions there was one creation, one history and one ending with the coming of the kingdom of god.

Second, in the old religions good and evil were relative. The gods were simply powers with whom one made compacts in order to gain the assistance of the gods in various endeavors. Good tended to be identified with doing one's duty to the gods, and evil with neglecting it. One god's goodness might be another god's evil. Most important, however, was that this attitude caused most worshippers of the old religions to be tolerant and often quite respectful of the worship of other gods. There were no heresies, no absolute definitions of good and evil.

The new religions changed all of that. Zoroastrianism was the first major state religion to characterize deviation as heresy. The Jews were known and resented throughout the ancient world for their lack of respect for other gods and for their attitude that they and only they had the truth. Traditional religions fused and mingled (syncretism) simply because all were regarded as various paths to the truth. But the Jews and the offshoots of Judaism were exclusivist. In the new religions the idea of the dialectic between Good and Evil became a central theme.

There was one tendency found in many of the old religions that carried over into these new religions. This was the idea that the material world is a sinful place and that one must transcend it and address oneself entirely to the concerns of a higher level of spirituality on another plane of being. The new religions carried this idea to unprecedented levels. One group, the Gnostics, believed that this world had been created by the powers of darkness and was wholly sinful. Christianity also was to adhere to this view to some extent. This contributed, for example, to the negative attitude of St. Paul toward women. In his view, women, the agents of childbirth, brought new people into this world and caused more sparks of pure divine fire to be trapped on this plane of gross matter.

Now let us look at the eastern fish. It is perpendicular to the ecliptic, swimming north away from the ecliptic. If we visualize the ecliptic as the symbol of the material world of space and time, we see the eastern fish as the symbol of a soul trying to ascend out of this world into a higher plane of manifestation. At the same time, there are two fish tied together by a single knot. This is a symbol of conflict and polarization between the eastern fish trying to ascend out of this plane, and the western fish, which is swimming parallel to the ecliptic and symbolizes the effort to move within and to understand the material universe. Here in the morphomaton itself is a symbol of the conflict between absolute Good and Evil.

The vertical, eastern fish not only can be viewed as a symbol of the soul trying to transcend the physical plane and ascend to a higher, spiritual level, it can also be viewed as a symbol of the world as organized hierarchically from the highest, most spiritual and most powerful, to the lowest, most material and most subjugated. Social hierarchy was nothing new at this time, but this symbol certainly reinforces it. It is very interesting that if we take that western fish and its length of cord and move it back to the vertical axis of the eastern fish and its cord, we have the symbol of the cross. Pisces, the morphomaton, symbolizes the age of the struggle of the polarity of spirit and matter, Good and Evil. One must turn one's back on nature if one is to be wholly good. It is this idea of the physical plane being sinful merely because it is physical that is peculiar to this time. The old paganism had a healthy respect and high regard for the natural world.

If the morphomaton of Pisces is the symbol of the dialectic between a thesis and an antithesis, then these new religions are the thesis. What then is the antithesis? As soon as Christianity became the dominant member of this group of new religions, it defined the antithesis. It called it the Antichrist.

Returning once again to the progression of Pisces, the first age of the Piscean Age is the age of the eastern fish. It extends, as we have already seen, from 111 B.C. to 371 A.D. What happened in history around 371 A.D.? In 380 A.D. Theodosius the Great, the last emperor of the united Roman Empire, declared that Christianity was the sole legal religion of the Empire. All citizens of the Empire had to subscribe to a single creed, the creed of orthodox, Catholic Christianity, the church that is still with us today. In fact, Theodosius in his documents was the first to use the term Catholic.

So in the first era of the Piscean Age we move from the spiritual ferment that gave birth to Christianity, to the birth of Christianity itself and its codification with Paul, to its being one of a large group of mystical, spiritual religions, to its triumph under Constantine the Great and its complete conquest of all rivals under Theodosius. The era of the eastern fish brought forth a tremendous burst of spiritual energy resulting in the creation of one of the world's greatest and most peculiar religions.

But as the vernal point moves further westward, the morphomaton becomes parallel to the ecliptic. This suggests that the period of spiritual creativity is over and what remains is simply the spreading of the new religion over a larger area.

Where does Islam fit into this? Islam is part of the spreading process. Islam is theologically quite different from Christianity in particulars, but it shares all of the main characteristics of the "new religions" as described above. It must be noted that Jesus' teachings were not the most important aspect of Christianity as it came to be. The most important aspect of Christianity from the point of view of this discussion is its intolerance of heresy, its emphasis on the polarity of Good and Evil and its emphasis on linear history from Creation to Fall to final triumph of the Good. From this broad perspective, Islam is simply substituting Mohammed for Jesus of Nazareth. Islam views the Old Testament as a sacred work and even accepts Jesus as one of the prophets. Islam and Christianity are sister religions born of the Zoroastrian-Judaic tradition. The spread of Islam throughout the world, sometimes even at the expense of Christianity, is simply part of the vernal point moving along the cord of the western fish.

However, as we shall see, the most important developments of the Piscean Age are to be found in the West, and it is here that the synchronicity works best. And shortly we shall see why the West is so important.

The year 1351 is the midpoint of the Piscean Age as defined by the morphomaton. At this point history is exactly halfway between the onset of the eastern fish and the end of the western fish. Where are we in European history? We are at the beginning of the Renaissance. We are also at a time when the official Christian institution, the Roman Catholic Church, began to lose its grip. In England there was the largely anticlerical Peasants' Revolt. Also in England John Wyclif preached for the reform of the church and began the Lollard movement, a movement that was instrumental in paving the way for Protestantism in England. In France the Papacy was held virtual prisoner at Avignon, which caused a great loss of respect for the Papacy in other countries. This finally culminated in the Great Schism of 1378 to 1417.

However, the most significant development within the Italian Renaissance was the rebirth of Humanism. It is clear that the nineteenth century overplayed the idea of the Renaissance as a rebirth of culture. But it is also clear that it was the beginning of a great turning away from the ideals of the eastern fish. Then, of course, in the century following we have the beginnings of the Age of Exploration, which amounted to the largest expansion of European culture in history. The movement of culture and consciousness is increasingly along the horizontal, i.e. to investigate this world rather than concentrate upon the next. In the years ahead there was a turning back to eastern-fish consciousness with the Protestant reformation of the sixteenth century and its increased emphasis on spirituality. But in fact this only serves to weaken the old order further and pave the way for the era of the western fish.

In the later Middle Ages and early Renaissance many seers and prophets began to think that the era of the Antichrist was approaching. This is not too remarkable because people had been forecasting the arrival of the Antichrist for years. It was quite conventional in the Middle Ages to accuse the rulers of your opposing army or political faction of being the Antichrist. However, what makes the predictions of Pierre D'Ailly and Nostradamus so intriguing is that they specify the year. Pierre D'Ailly in 1414 predicted the appearance of the Antichrist in 1789 and Nostradamus predicted the appearance in 1792. Nostradamus is quite specific in describing a return of paganism. Of course these are the years of the French Revolution. On November 10, 1793, the royal chapel at St. Denis was reinstituted as a temple of the goddess Reason, and Christianity was abolished.

Even more significant for our purposes is that in 1793 the vernal point was only 20 minutes of arc from the tail of the western fish. If, as we have stated, the eastern fish is the thesis, then the era of the western fish should indeed be the era of the antithesis. And what is the Antithesis of Christ but Antichrist? So has the Antichrist come? I believe the answer is yes, but that this does not mean what tradition has said that it means. Tradition, after all, is "Christian," i.e. dominated by the church founded by Saint Paul and officially established by the edicts of Constantine and Theodosius. If Christianity and Islam are, as the "new religions" described earlier, the thesis, then an antithesis of those new religions should have come into being at about the time Nostradamus and D'Ailly predicted. Just as the "new religions" are not in fact the religion of one person but the creations of many during several hundred years, the Antichrist would also not be one person, but a system of ideas. And just as there were individuals (like Jesus, Paul, Mohammed and Augustine) who had strong influence upon the Christian-Islamic thesis, so there would be individuals who would particularly embody the anti-religion. But first let us look at the symbolism of the morphomaton of Pisces to get further insights into this.

The West Fish

We have already shown that the west fish swims toward the west, away from the east fish, which swims north. It swims parallel to the ecliptic. This symbolism suggests moving along and abroad on the material plane rather than trying to transcend into another world. Thus, if the east fish symbolizes the transcendence of the material, the west fish symbolizes extension within it. Yet the west fish is tied to the east fish at a common knot at Alpha Piscium. It is significant that the constellation starts with the knot rather than with either of the two fish themselves. The basic underlying symbolic statement of Pisces precedes either of its two poles. It is probably a coincidence, given the fact that the Greek-letter designations of the fixed stars were assigned in modern times, but it remains true that the era of the eastern fish starts with Alpha Piscium and the era of the western fish starts with Omega Piscium. In the Book of Revelation the figure whom St. John interprets as the Christ states, "I am the Alpha and the Omega." It seems especially significant in view of the fact that the alpha star of a constellation is supposed to be the brightest star in the constellation, yet Alpha Piscium is not, due to an error made in the original brightness determination. (Of course, it is possible that its brightness may have changed in the last few hundred years.) I realize that this might seem to be stretching the long arm of coincidence, but the whole point here is that it is just this sort of meaningful coincidence that is the backbone of this kind of interpretation. We are using our projection of psychic contents upon the fixed stars and all of the symbolism associated with them to gain relevant information about the evolution of our culture.

This coincidence (the Alpha and Omega), the starting of the age of Pisces with the knot, and the fact that the two fish are tied together at a common point tell us something very important about Christ and Antichrist. They have an underlying unity. They are not total opposites but rather polar manifestations of the same basic principles. In order to see this more clearly we have to formulate more clearly what the Antichrist is.

The major shift that occurred in the time immediately before and after the beginning of the era of the second fish (1817 A.D.) was from a religiously ordered society to a secular one. For a time, the Protestant Reformation looked as if it would be a resurgence of the eastern-fish kind of religion, but what the Reformation chiefly served to do was to weaken the authority of tradition to such an extent that a radically new way of thinking could come into being.

The energy of the Reformation destroyed itself on the shoals of the Thirty Years' War (1618-1648). What started out as a religious war between Protestants and the Catholic reaction became, before it was over, merely a war between various European powers with purely secular motives. Whereas prior to the Thirty Years' War there was a tremendous resurgence of mysticism, after the war, movement toward the Age of Reason began, culminating in the enthronement of the goddess Reason in her temple in 1793. The Scientific Revolution also began in this period. And from the mid-eighteenth century on, the Industrial Revolution begins. All of these are factors that are instrumental in transforming the era of the Christ into the era of the Antichrist. And of course shortly after 1817 came the beginning of Marxist Scientific Socialism, or Communism, which many seem to believe is the epitome of the Antichrist. However, I would also include Capitalism as being an equal manifestation. Let us look at the role of each of these.

The Age of Reason and the Scientific Revolution are, of course, two aspects of the same movement. It is noteworthy that both of these have their roots in countries such as Britain and France, where a strong monarchy had deprived the Church of much of its power. Both of these movements tended to displace revelation and authority with individual observation and experiment. The word of prophets and inspired saints began to be held less worthy than scientific observation. However, scientific observation being what it is, only the physical world could be examined. The inner world of the spirit began to pale beside not only science, but any form of observation. Religion was tolerated, but theology came to be considered a very inferior form of knowledge.

The idea of a monarchic creator whose constant interference was necessary to maintain existence was gradually displaced by Natural Law. Finally when Laplace was asked by Napoleon where God fit into his theory of the universe, Laplace replied, "I have no need of that hypothesis." One could choose to believe in God or not, but there was little that compelled one to do so.

The ideal of the Second Coming, the Millenium and even heaven in an afterlife came to be replaced by the theory of progress and the belief in a future on earth that would be perfect. Of course, the kicker here is that individuals alive on earth now will never get to see this future civilization because they will be dead. Nevertheless, the ideal of progress has managed to play essentially the same role for modern times that the heavenly city played in the Middle Ages.

The Industrial Revolution depended for its ideology on the progress ideal but it also introduced a new ethic. Instead of a morality based on revelation, it had a morality based on practical necessity. Christian morality was invoked only when it served the needs of the ruling classes. When it did not, it was violated freely. This is what caused Marx to note that religion was the opiate of the people, i.e. that which served to tranquilize them so that they would not get upset and revolutionary. During the Industrial Revolution, organized Christianity became the tool of the very power that it originally opposed.

The Industrial Revolution also displaced God as a historical force with Economic Necessity, paving the way for Marx, who made the most nearly perfect statement of the religion of the Antichrist. In Marxism the heavenly city is replaced by the idealized classless society. The battle between good and evil is replaced by dialectical materialism, and economic forces are the only recognized forces of history. It is interesting to note that Marxism has even created an orthodox theology, departures from which are treated as heresy and persecuted as enthusiastically as any oldtime church. However, again it must be said that Marxism has no corner on being an antichristian philosophy.

All of the above factors have given rise to a new worldview in which matter is primary and spirit secondary. Life is treated as a secondary consequence of the laws that govern inanimate matter and energy. Consciousness has become merely the result of environmental forces. Instead of spirit, mechanism is the basis for all interactions among entities. Capitalism by its vigorous sponsorship of the mechanist-materialist worldview and its treatment of people as parts of an industrial apparatus is every bit as antichristian as Marxism. In fact, it is more similar than different from Marxism in most of these regards. But it is cleverer in its treatment of religion, in that instead of suppressing it, which always makes religion grow stronger, it tries to use it for its own ends and supports all religion which does so. The current alliance between right-wing Christian fundamentalism and Capitalism demonstrates the point nicely. Here we see the alleged followers of a religion that is completely opposed to mechanist-materialism operating as some of its most vigorous supporters.

The new order is, however, not all bad. The energy of the Antichrist is not any more intrinsically evil than that of what we have called the "Christ." It is simply its antithesis. For example, the arrangement of the eastern and western fish with respect to the ecliptic suggests something else besides what we have already mentioned. Not only does the vertical placement of the east fish suggest concern with the spritual world, the world of transcendence, it also suggests a world that is organized hierarchically, with the Emperor and Pope at the top, the kings and lords at the next level, and so forth down to the lowest peasant. This was in fact the structure of European society in the Middle Ages.

Now, however, in the era of the west fish we have democratic states, and even where democracy is not respected, social egalitariansim is an ideal even when honored only in the breach. Even in the Soviet Union complete social equality is the alleged goal of the system. Of course, this can also lead to a blurring of real distinctions among people as well as a blurring of the artificial ones of birth and social background. But egalitarianism as a characteristic of the era of the west fish does give us some hope.

While we are into creative coincidences, there is another that might be worth mentioning, the phenomenon of East and West from the point of view of Western consciousness. The era of the eastern fish was dominated by Eastern culture. Christianity, itself, comes from the Near East. And through the entire period after the fall of Rome in the West, most of the cultural activity in the world took place in the East: Arabia, India and China. But as the vernal point moved west, so did culture. Arabic culture, which dominated the early Middle Ages, began to lose its dominance as Islamic fundamentalism brought the scientific and philosophical innovation of the Arab world to a halt. Also at about this time in the late Middle Ages, the Arab world became weakened by the invasions of the Turks and Mongols, similar to the barbarian invasions that had crippled the West in the fifth century A.D. Byzantium, the last outpost of Greco-Roman civilization, fell in 1453, well after the vernal point had gotten halfway through the morphomaton.

From Italy, the Renaissance moved west to the Atlantic shore, to France and Great Britain. And then across the Atlantic to America, and in the case of the U.S., at least, across the American continent. It is interesting to note that the westward motion is continuing: much of the current industrial ascendancy of Japan can be traced directly to what the Japanese have gotten from the U.S. While we think of the U.S. as a Western nation and of Japan as an Eastern nation, the actual flow of energy has been westward across the Pacific. This, however, is not to be understood as failing to recognize that Japan has had a long and brilliant career of its own as a civilization. It is merely its technology (and baseball) that has come from the West.

The Knot

We have already noted that the two fish are bound at the knot, Alpha Piscium. We have suggested that this indicates an underlying connection between the apparent polarity of the east and west fish. The two fish have strong similarities, some of which have already been noted.

The philosophies of both the east and west fish seek a better world than this one, the east fish in heaven, the west fish in the future. Both philosophical systems are intolerant of heresies and regard deviant opinions as manifestations of fundamental evil. And of course, the idea of the struggle between Good and Evil is as fundamental now as it has ever been.

But there is another similarity that has often been overlooked, which truly ties the two eras together and also represents the greatest flaw of both eras. The Jewish God was not normally conceived as immanent, that is, as being part of the nature that he had created. Yahweh is an ego, bigger and more powerful than a human being, but an ego nevertheless. Except for certain religions and philosophies not of the mainstream, most taught that Good was apart from Man as well as Nature. Among the non-mainstream believers was probably Jesus himself. Both in the Gospel of St. John and the non-canonic gospels (this is in fact what made them non-canonic) we see clear indications that Jesus believed that God was a part of Man. However, the teachings of St. Paul have almost completely obscured this aspect of Christianity. It has been revived again and again, however, most notably by St. Francis of Assisi and the Society of Friends.

The importance of this from our standpoint is that the view of God as totally transcendent and external to Man places all truth outside of the individual. Truth is seen from a God's-eye perspective. In the era of the east fish, truth may be derived only from God's word as established by the Church and Bible. In the era of the west fish, God has ceased to play an obvious role in defining truth, but it still remains that truth is determined from a God's-eye point of view. This is essentially what is meant by objectivity as employed in the sciences. Individual experience is characterized as mere subjectivity, and lack of involvement is considered a prerequisite for judgment. This is called "being objective." Thus we have teachers teaching subjects they have never practiced, celibate experts on marriage and family living, and the whole panoply of uninvolved experts. But most significantly, we have a culture of people who do not trust their own experience, nor do they know how to interpret it, nor do they even believe it to be real. A second consequence of this problem is the Western attitude toward nature. We regard ourselves as apart from nature, and nature as something to be ruthlessly exploited and conquered. In the era of the east fish we had Christian missionaries chopping down sacred groves that had stood for thousands of years, and in the era of the west fish we have officials to whom a wilderness is a "parking lot without lines." Science (or more precisely scientism) and mechanist-materialism in the era of the west fish come directly from the Judaic-Christian-Islamic philosophies of the era of the east fish.

In this time there are many currents that seem to define a new antithesis to the thesis of mechanist-materialism. It is this fact that has led so many to postulate that we are entering a new age, the Age of Aquarius. Obviously I do not agree that the Piscean Age is over. But I do believe that there really are important changes taking place. What are they?

To begin with, it is clear that the era of the west fish is firmly established. In the eighteenth and nineteenth centuries the symbolism of the west fish had to become established in the face of the remaining energies of the east fish and the long transitional era that followed. But this process is complete. The symbolism of the west fish has wiped out some aspects of the east fish and formed a synthesis with others. Examples of this have been mentioned above. Now we have two possibilities. We can re-react against the west fish and retreat to more primitive forms of cultural expression, or we can move to create a new antithesis that challenges and at the same time balances the tendencies of the west fish. Examples of the first type of response abound. We have masses of people in both the Islamic and Christian world who have reverted to the oldest, least rational and probably least conscious forms of religious expression that their religions have to offer. They do so out of a sense that the new order has undermined basic human values that they hold important. And they are right. But at the same time they unleash forces of aggression, intolerance and inhumanity as they seek to preserve an aspect of their humanity from new forces.

We also see the forces of retrogression in those who fear new technology and seek to withdraw into pretechnological ways of life. This is a very powerful element within the counter-culture. But these attempts to return to the past cannot remedy the evils that have given rise to them. Those who seek to return to old religious forms are usually co-opted by the system that they seek to undo (again, the alliance between fundamentalist Christians and Capitalism) and the others are simply ineffective. Both groups become infected very rapidly with self-righteousness. Their in-groups possess all goodness, and the enemy is totally evil. The Islamic fundamentalists of Iran actually accuse America of being the "Great Satan," whereas America is merely the agent of the energies of the west fish. Many individuals in the counter-culture regard the government as the tool of an evil conspiracy. The point here is simply that these people are once again retreating into the dualism of the Piscean Age. By reinforcing that dualism they make growth beyond this dualism impossible.

We need a new way of looking at the world that transcends the limitations of the entire Piscean age, not merely the latest part of it. It must go beyond Good and Evil, beyond the limited idea of history and beyond the terrible split between Humanity and Nature. The goals must be consciousness and love. The first allows us to see what truly is and the second allows us to embrace it joyfully. If we have nearly nine hundred years of the era of the west fish to go through before we completely reach the Age of Aquarius, then we have nothing better to do than to infuse history with love and consciousness.

Acknowledgements

"The Moon, the Four Phases of the Feminine." *Aquarian Agent*, July 1972. Reprinted with the permission of Astrology Services International, Inc.

"The Wave Theory of Astrology." From a lecture delivered to the National Council for Geocosmic Research meeting in New York City on November 30, 1973.

"Mercury, the Modulator." From the *Journal of Geocosmic Research*, Vol. 1, No. 2, 1975. Reprinted with permission of the American Federation of Astrologers.

"Handling the Malefics." From *Kósmos*: the Quarterly Publication of ISAR, Vol. 9, No. 4, Fall 1980. Reprinted with the permission of the International Society for Astrological Research, Inc.

"Geocentric Latitude: Some Second Thoughts." From the *Journal of Geocosmic Research*, Vol. 2, No. 1, 1976. Reprinted with the permission of the National Council for Geocosmic Research, Inc.

"On Creating a Science of Astrology." From the *Journal of Geocosmic Research*, Vol. 2, No. 1, 1976. Reprinted with the permission of the National Council for Geocosmic Research, Inc.

"A New Approach to Transits." From *Cosmecology Bulletin*, June 1976. Reprinted with permission of the Association for Research in Cosmecology.

"Crises of Human Growth." *Astrology Now*, Vol. 3, No. 20, June 1978. As originally published in *Astrology Now* by Llewellyn Publications, St. Paul, Minn. Reprinted with kind permission by *Astrology Now*, a subsidiary of TYL Associates Incorporated.

"Astrology's Second Dimension: Declination and Latitude." Vol. 4, No. 1, April/May 1979. As originally published in *Astrology Now* by Llewellyn Publications, St. Paul, Minn. Reprinted with kind permission by *Astrology Now*, a subsidiary of TYL Associates Incorporated.

"Symbols of the Father Complex." From *Kósmos*, Vol. 10, No. 4, Fall 1981. Reprinted with permission of the International Society for Astrological Research, Inc.

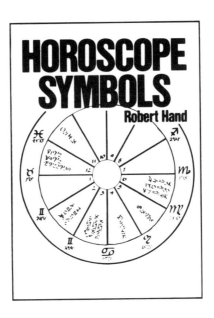

HOROSCOPE SYMBOLS

Robert Hand

Horoscope Symbols, Para Research's latest book by leading astrologer Robert Hand, explores astrological symbolism. Hand, with twenty years experience in the field, analyzes traditional meanings, considers alternatives and uses his own experience to develop and clarify these symbols. He thoroughly explains astrological symbolism—its history as well as its application for modern astrologers. In this new work, Robert Hand continues to build his reputation as the major new voice in humanistic astrology.

   The author covers such basics as signs, planets, houses and aspects, illuminating their core meanings. In addition, Hand discusses midpoints, harmonics, the effect of retrograde planets and other often confusing areas for the astrologer.

   Previously announced as *Planets in Synthesis, Horoscope Symbols* is the culmination of four years work. If you are new to astrology, this is the book to grow with. If you have already studied the basics, Robert Hand's approach will give you new perspective, insight and wisdom.

   To quote the noted astrologer Alan Oken reviewing Robert Hand's *Horoscope Symbols:* " As usual, his writing is very clear, . . . what is most noteworthy is his ability to synthesize his comprehensive understanding of astrology from his basic scientific viewpoint . . . in humanistic prose.

ISBN 0-914918-16-8
371 pages, 6½″ x 9¼″, paper

$19.95

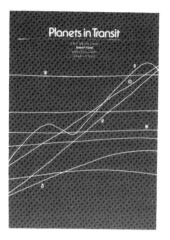

PLANETS IN YOUTH
Patterns of Early
Development

Robert Hand

In this book, a major astrologer looks at children and childhood.

As Hand says in his introduction, "...the child as an adult in the process of becoming is the orientation that this book takes."

Not only will parents welcome this book, readers of all ages will use it to understand their own patterns of early development.

The first four chapters discuss parental influences, explain the effects of various planetary energy systems and explore the meanings of all the different factors in a child's chart. There are interpretations of charts of three children, including Judy Garland and Shirley Temple.

The major part of the book consists of 300-word delineations of horoscope factors. Every planet in every sign and house, as well as in every major aspect, is interpreted in language that emphasizes possibilities.

ISBN 0-914918-26-5
367 pages, 6½" x 9¼", paper   **$18.95**

PLANETS IN TRANSIT
Life Cycles for Living

Robert Hand

This is *the* definitive work on transiting planets. Its psychological insight and completeness as a reference book have brought Robert Hand recognition as a leading astrologer. Hand takes a humanistic, multi-leveled approach to transits: the events that may happen, the feelings you may experience, and the possibilities of each transit for growth and awareness.

This book covers complete delineations of all the major transits— conjunction, sextile, square, trine and opposition—that occur between transiting Sun, Moon and all planets to each planet in the natal chart and the Ascendant and Midheaven, as well as complete delineations of each planet transiting each house of the natal chart. These 720 lucid delineations are full of insight for both the professional astrologer and the beginner.

ISBN 0-914918-24-9
524 pages, 6½" x 9¼", paper   **$24.95**

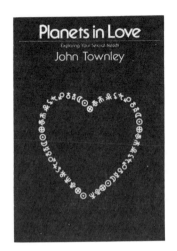

PLANETS IN COMPOSITE
Analyzing Human Relationships
Robert Hand

Robert Hand has written an important reference book that is much needed in the astrological field, a definitive work about human relationships.

After extensive research and professional experience, Hand has concluded that the composite chart technique works more effectively than other techniques as a method of interpreting relationships.

Planets in Composite, now in paperback, contains an introduction to casting and reading the composite chart, five case studies and twelve chapters of delineations. You will find 374 interpretations of composite planetary positions including forty-one delineations of the Moon's nodes.

Planets in Composite is the most authoritative book ever written about the astrology of human relationships.

ISBN 0-914918-22-2
362 pages, 6½" x 9¼", paper **$19.95**

PLANETS IN LOVE
Exploring Your Emotional and Sexual Needs
John Townley

This is the first major astrological work to take a direct and detailed look at human sexuality. It explores the variety of relationships people form to satisfy their individual emotional and sexual needs.

An intimate analysis of sex and love, *Planets in Love* is not a collection of chatty commentaries on paired Sun signs but 550 in-depth delineations of all planetary positions by sign, house and aspect.

In addition, the book includes numerous case studies illustrating the use of the natal chart in interpreting an individual's unique expression of love.

This is a mature text that takes a sophisticated approach to love, sex and sexuality. Now in paperback.

ISBN 0-914918-11-7
368 pages, 6½" x 9¼", paper **$18.95**

PLANETS IN HOUSES
Experiencing Your Environment

Robert Pelletier

This major work, now in paperback, brings natal horoscope interpretation to a new level of accuracy, concreteness and richness of detail.

While the fundamental forces at work in a chart can be found in the relationships of the planets, signs and aspects, it is the houses that bring chart-reading down to earth, indicating how planetary energies will work themselves out in daily life.

Pelletier synthesizes the meaning of each planet in each house—as derived by counting from each of the houses and in relation to each of the other houses with which it forms trines, sextiles, squares, oppositions, inconjuncts and semisextiles.

So if you've been waiting for the definitive work on house meanings, a book that will both encourage the beginner and challenge the expert, this is the book for you.

ISBN 0-914918-27-3
366 pages, 6½" x 9¼", paper **$19.95**

PLANETS IN ASPECT
Understanding Your Inner Dynamics

Robert Pelletier

"Robert Pelletier has presented the world with a mighty volume of mature, erudite and modern aspect delineations...Delineations by Pelletier embrace a large portion of every aspect's spectrum of potential manifestation..."
—Noel Tyl, *Gnostic News*

There have been many books written about astrology, but the subject of aspects has often been overlooked or treated too lightly. *Planets in Aspect* is a book every astrologer needs: a complete reference work on planetary aspects.

Pelletier delineates 314 aspects; every major aspect between planet is covered: conjunction, sextile, square, trine, opposition and inconjunct with 300 words devoted to each aspect.

Planets in Aspect, now in paperback, is the most thorough study of aspects ever published.

ISBN 0-914918-20-6
364 pages, 6½" x 9¼", paper **$19.95**

ASTROLOGY INSIDE OUT

Bruce Nevin

Besides being an excellent introduction to astrology, *Astrology Inside Out* is an entirely new way of approaching this timeless discipline. Bruce Nevin uses a traditional theoretic framework combined with a modern harmonic research and recent developments in physics and psychology to produce a book that will fascinate and challenge all serious students of astrology.

Before even approaching the horoscope, Nevin teaches the reader to translate the events and circumstances of life into the symbolic language of astrology. The circle of houses and its contents become vivid realities and tools for interpreting experiences, solving problems and resolving conflicts.

Then, the book builds on the knowledge you've gained to help you understand the art of horoscope delineation in greater depth. You then learn to identify the contribution of each sign's ruler, exaltation, detriment and fall in a unique analytical format. Through this method, sources of strength are easily identified in each individual horoscope.

And beyond all this, *Astrology Inside Out* teaches you to use meditation to achieve further understanding of the chart so that you can really learn astrology from the "inside out."

ISBN 0-914918-19-2
320 pages, 6½" x 9¼", paper

$18.95

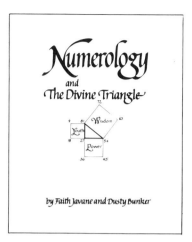

NUMEROLOGY & THE DIVINE TRIANGLE

Faith Javane & Dusty Bunker

Now in its fifth printing, this major work embodies the life's work of Faith Javane, one of America's most respected numerologists, and her student and co-author Dusty Bunker, a teacher and columnist on metaphysical topics.

Part I introduces esoteric numerology. Topics include: the digits 1 through 9; how to derive your personal numbers from your name and date of birth; how to chart your life path; the symbolism of each letter in the alphabet; the life of Edgar Cayce, and more.

Part II delineates the numbers 1 through 78 and, illustrated with the Rider-Waite Tarot deck, synthesizes numerology, astrology and the Tarot. *Numerology & The Divine Triangle* is number one in its field.

ISBN 0-914918-10-9
266 pages, 6½" x 9¼", paper $14.95

NUMEROLOGY AND YOUR FUTURE

Dusty Bunker

In her second book, Dusty Bunker stresses the predictive side of numerology. Personal cycles, including yearly, monthly and even daily numbers are explored as the author presents new techniques for revealing future developments. Knowledge of these cycles will help you make decisions and take actions in your life.

In addition to the extended discussion of personal cycles, the numerological significance of decades is analyzed with emphasis on the particular importance of the 1980s. Looking toward the future, the author presents a series of examples from the past, particularly the historical order of American presidents in relation to keys from the Tarot, to illustrate the power of numbers. Special attention is paid to the twenty-year death cycle of the presidents, as well as several predictions for the presidential elections.

ISBN 0-914918-18-4
235 pages, 6½" x 9¼", paper $14.95